More than 100 years... and growing

Leigh Michaels
Michael W. Lemberger

PBL Limited
Ottumwa Iowa

South Ottumwa Savings Bank
Copyright 2014 by Leigh Michaels & Michael W. Lemberger

Cover illustration and design copyright 2014
by Michael W. Lemberger

This edition published 2014 for South Ottumwa Savings Bank

10 9 8 7 6 5 4 3 2 1

ISBN 13: 978-1501078972

Printed in the United States of America

Cover photograph and illustrations on pages 6, 7, 13, 14, 23, 28, 29, 30, 31, 32, 33, 34, 35, 36, 38, 44, 45, 46, 47, 52, 53, 54, 58, 60, 100-101, 104, 105, 106, 107, 108, 109, 110, 112: Courtesy of **The Lemberger Collection**. For more information about the collection of historic photos, which has been called the largest and best-documented privately-owned photography collection in the world, visit www.mlemberger.com.

Illustrations not listed above are from South Ottumwa Savings Bank archives or employees' personal collections and are used with permission, or are photographs of items in the South Ottumwa Savings Bank collections or in employee's personal collections, and are used with permission.

All rights reserved. Except for brief passages quoted in any review, the reproduction or utilization of this work in whole or in part, in any form or by any electronic, mechanical, or other means, now known or hereinafter invented, including xerography, photocopying and recording, or in any information storage and retrieval system, is forbidden without the express permission of the publisher. For permission contact:

Rights Editor
PBL Limited
P.O. Box 935
Ottumwa IA 52501-0935
pbl@pbllimited.com

Visit www.pbllimited.com for more information.

SOUTH
Ottumwa
SAVINGS BANK

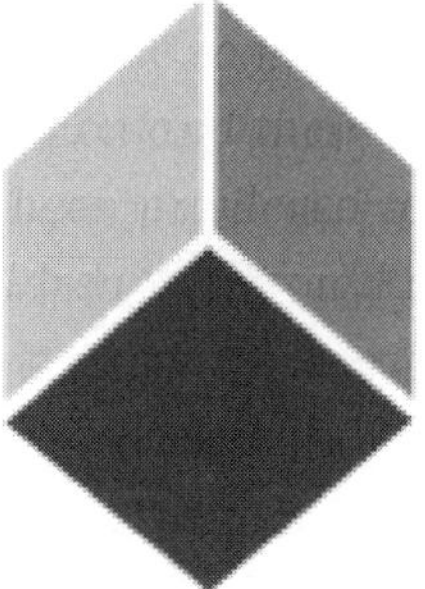

To our customers
past, present and future

and

To our employees
past, present and future

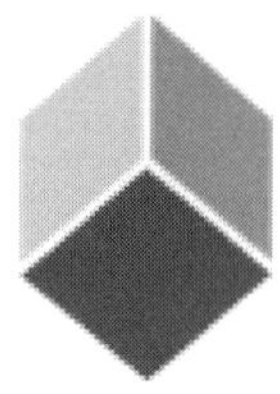

Timeline

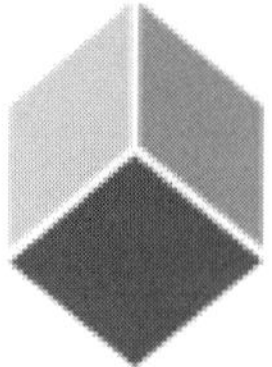

1903 Bank established as a currency exchange on the site that is presently South Side Drug, with W. A. McIntire as president

1907 C. D. Evans becomes cashier upon the retirement of J. V. Curran

1908 Frank McIntyre is elected President

1910 Bank receives its charter from the state as a savings institution, in January

---

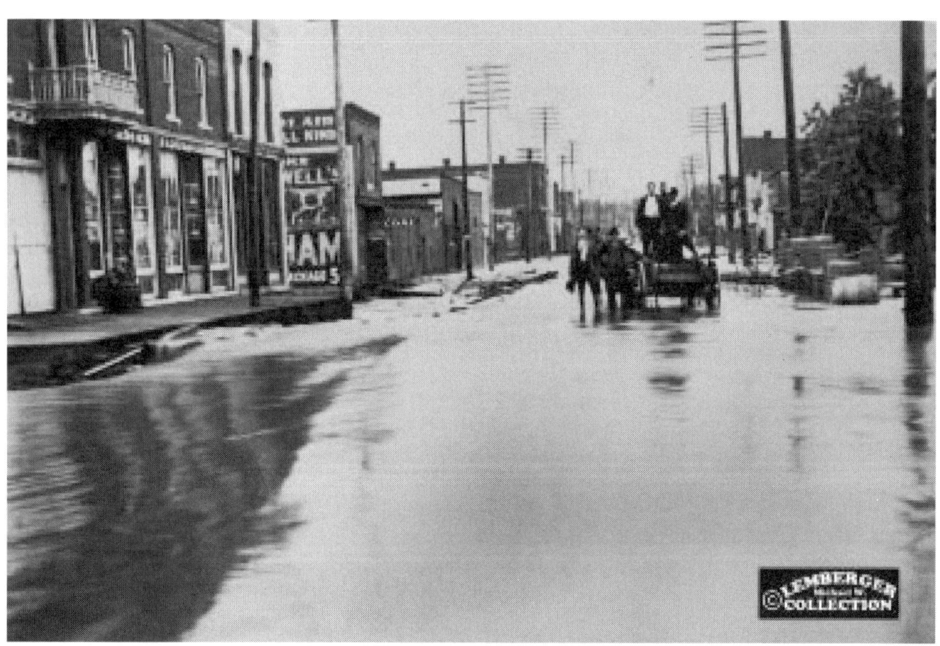

Flood of June 1903 on Church Street in South Ottumwa, looking toward the river from Ransom Street.

Aftermath of the flood of June 1903 on Church Street from the intersection of Sheridan Street. South Ottumwa Savings Bank, founded in 1903, was initally located in one of the buildings at center left. The present location of the bank is behind the awning at center. G.W. Baldwin's bicycle repair shop, at right, was located at 416 Church Street.

1910 South Ottumwa Savings Bank is incorporated on February 18, 1910

1912 New building erected at the corner of Weller & Church, where the main bank is presently located

1922 Ralph Watson joins the Bank

1955 Myron Ackley is elected to the Board of Directors

South Ottumwa Savings Bank

This metal bank is probably from the Ottumwa Savings Bank, located at Main and Court Streets on the north side of the river, rather than from South Ottumwa Savings Bank. The two banks are often confused by historians and collectors because of the similar names and the fact that physical addresses were seldom included in ads or on products.

1955 Bank building is remodeled

1956 Robert Ackley, son of Myron, joins the Bank

1957 C. D. Evans retires from the Bank and the Board of Directors

1958 H. H. Evans retires from the Bank and the Board of Directors

1959 Lot next to the Main Bank, which housed the Do Drop Inn, is purchased

1964 Original building is removed and existing building is constructed

1970 Robert Ackley elected President

1976 Ralph Watson retires from the Bank after 53 years

1976 Penn-Elm Bank is opened at the intersection of Pennsylvania and Elm, the first branch north of the river

1980 Motor Bank is opened at 501 North Weller

1982 Two-story addition is added to the Main Bank, constructed on the original bank building location

1985 M. L. Ackley retires from the Bank after 30 years

1986 Robert Ackley becomes Chairman of the Board

1986 South Ottumwa Savings Bank becomes a wholly owned subsidiary of South Ottumwa Bancshares, Inc.

1987 Robert Ackley retires from the Bank after 31 years

1987 Phil Drumm becomes President/CEO, Don Roemerman becomes Chairman of the Board

1990 Sunshine Society Club is established as a travel and event club for seniors

1992 Bank purchases assets of Peoples Federal Savings Association

1994 Bank purchases parking lot behind the Main Bank to expand customer parking

1995 New addition is added to Main Bank in order to relocate Loan Department, Ag Department and Sunshine Club

1996 An airplane accident takes the lives of Bank President Phil Drumm and Board Director David Carpenter, along with two other Ottumwa businessmen, William Dew and Jerry Yetley

1996 Don Roemerman becomes acting president

1997 Thomas M. Awtry becomes President/CEO

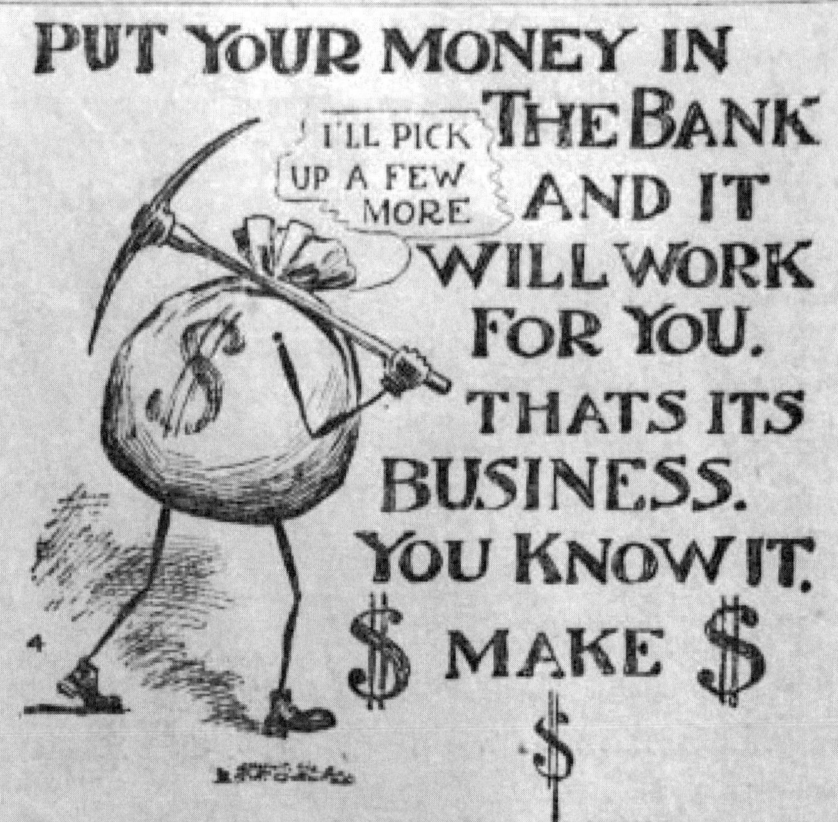

This ad was run in 1908 by the Ottumwa Savings Bank, located at Main and Court Streets, not by the South Ottumwa Savings Bank -- but the philosophy expressed was common for the time: Save a dollar a day and in twenty years the compounded amount "will support you the rest of your life".

1997 Don Roemerman retires from the Bank after 43 years

1998 Major remodeling occurs at the Main Bank

1999 Remodeling occurs at the Penn-Elm Bank

2000 The Penn-Elm Bank remodeling is completed

2000 South Ottumwa Bancshares, Inc. becomes Cornerstone Financial Services Group, Inc.

2001 Ground breaking takes place for the North Court Bank at 2525 North Court Road

2002 The North Court Bank is completed, with grand opening April 1, 2002

2003 South Ottumwa Savings Bank celebrates 100 years

2008 South Ottumwa Savings Bank purchases Fareway property at 316 Church Street, allowing expansion of the Main Bank

2011 South Ottumwa Savings Bank purchases Hedrick Savings Bank

2012 Thomas M. Awtry retires from the Bank after 15 years

2013 Teri Messerschmitt becomes President/CEO

2014 New addition to Main Bank is completed and the 1964 building is renovated

---

The phones at SOSB were answered by a person – and that has not changed.

— Nancy McWilliams

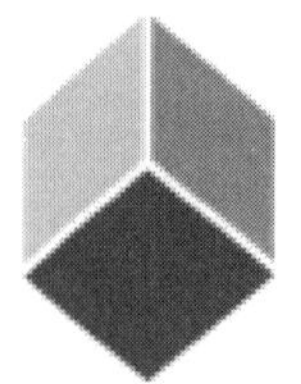

Banking in the Old Days

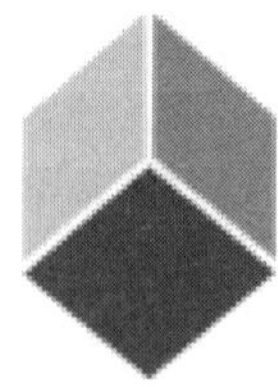

by Charles D. Evans
president of South Ottumwa Savings Bank
Published in the Ottumwa *Courier* (no date)

In May, 1904, Mr. Evans began work in the old Taylor-McGowan bank at Bloomfield, Iowa. Many years later he spoke of his experiences to a gathering of Rotary Club members:

In those days the youngest clerk did the janitor work, fired the furnace and was the general handyman about the building. It was also the duty of the junior clerk to clerk the farm sales for the bank's customers.

If you have ever attended a farm closing out sale, you know something of the technique. The sale would begin near the house in the back yard where numerous odds and ends would be sold. From there, the sale would move down a line in the barn lot where farm tools and accessories would be sold. In due time, the hog pens would be reached. The hogs would be sold, then sheep, if any, cattle, horses, corn and oats and lastly, hay in the stack.

The rule was to sell a stack of hay as a whole at so much per ton, the stack to be measured and the number of tons figured by the clerk after the sale was over.

There are as many ways of measuring and figuring the number of tons in a stack as there are people who do the figuring.

We developed a technique for measuring hay stacks which rarely failed in obtaining an equitable settlement between buyer and seller. The hay should always be measured just after the

Charles D. Evans, SOSB president until 1957, at his desk in the bank

sale for the day is over, in order that the purchaser may observe the process and satisfy himself that every step is properly carried out and the computation accurately made.

Let us suppose that Hank Jones is holding the sale and that Jake Smith has bought the hay in the stack at $7.65 per ton. Ask Hank to provide 100 feet or so of binder twine and a yardstick, and armed with these, set out for the stack. Do not hesitate or glance back for you can invariably be assured that from 12 to 15 or more of the sale attendants and bidders at the sale will attach themselves to your party in the capacity of unofficial observers, advisers, mathematicians, stack climbers, and general assistants.

Arrived at the stack, ask Hank or Jake to hold one end of the twine, and with his assistance proceed to measure the length of the stack. If Hank, the seller, assists you, subtract two feet from the length; if Jake, the buyer, holds the other end of the twine, add two feet. This is called the "fudging correction" and represents the distance the average buyer or seller will fudge on you. In like manner, obtain the width of the stack.

Then comes the most interesting dimension of all, the "overthrow". Procure a chunk of stove wood or other object of suitable weight, and attach to one end of the twine. Taking careful aim, hurl the weight over the stack, allowing plenty of force to be sure of clearing the stack. On the first trial you will have forgotten to hold the other end of the twine and the whole shooting match will go sailing majestically over the stack following the weight. This seeming untoward circumstance gives you an opportunity to exhibit a nice bit of finesse. Do not allow yourself to appear disconcerted, but remark jauntily, "Well, that gives us the correct range."

Send a boy to bring back the twine and weight, and proceed as before, this time retaining a firm hold upon the unweighted end of the twine. Nine times out of ten, you will be overcautious

Church Street in South Ottumwa, in 1910. South Ottumwa Savings Bank occupies the site of the two buildings at left.

on this second trial, and the weight, barely clearing the top of the stack, will become lodged under a stack weight about halfway down on the other side. Never overlook your technique; be sure to maintain your jaunty attitude and unruffled ease. Conceal a yawn with your left hand, ignoring the jibes of the spectators; or, if you feel that you must take some notice of them, a gesture of well-bred indifference is attained by placing your right thumb against the tip of your nose, fingers extended. This indicates to the crowd that it is well, and that the measuring of the stack is going forward exactly as you have planned it. They will fall back in respectful silence as you pass around to the other side of the stack.

There you will find a half dozen willing shoulders to support you as you dig about in the snow on the side of the stack for the weight. Most of this snow will cascade down the opening between your collar and the back of your neck at which juncture the really accomplished hay stack measurer will never be at a loss for words to fit the occasion. The rest is easy. Having dislodged the weight in such a way that it strikes your head on the way down, you proceed to obtain the overthrow, measuring from the foot of the stack on each side and adding or subtracting four feet in this instance, on account of the fact that your biased assistant is now on the other side of the stack and out of your sight.

Having noted down the various measurements, it is then considered good form for you to suggest that the party repair to the farm kitchen rather than complete your calculations outside in the cold. There you may expect to find the members of the family and a few neighbors partaking of doughnuts and coffee, and it is not too much to hope that you also will be invited to participate.

Fortifying yourself with a few doughnuts, proceed to cover one sheet of scratch paper and half of another with figures which you will be careful to make quite small and illegible in order that your neighbor at the table will not be able to decipher them.

Then, poising your cup of coffee in your left hand, assume an air of mystery and inquire of Hank, the seller of the hay: "Well,

Hank, how much hay do you say there is in that stack?" Hank will probably reply, "Oh, there'd ort to be right onto 10 ton I sh'd say." Whereupon, Jake Smith, the buyer, will snort indignantly: "Why there caint be moren eight tons at the outside." The computation is now complete. You thereupon state, "Well, boys, you're both wrong." If Hank Jones, the seller, owes a past due note at the bank, you say there is exactly 9 1/8 tons; if Jake Smith, the buyer, owes the past due note, you say there is exactly 8 7/8 tons. In many years of experience, this system proved uniformly successful."

The South Ottumwa Savings Bank building located at Church and Weller Streets. Though this photo is undated, it is an early view of the building, probably before 1930. The building, constructed in 1912, was torn down in 1964 after a larger bank was built next door.

SOUTH OTTUMWA SAVINGS BANK

The organization of the above named bank was due in a large measure to the first president, W. A. McIntire, who died in June, 1908, after serving five years as the head of the bank and of a hardware business that bore his name for many years, in South Ottumwa. The bank was organized in 1903, and with W. A. McIntire as president, B. A. Hand, cashier, and Mrs. L. B. Goldsberry, assistant cashier, opened its doors for public patronage on Church Street, where it remained until about a year ago, when a permanent home was occupied at the corner of Church and Weller streets. The building is one story in height, with a stone front on Church Street.

In 1908, when Mr. McIntire died, Frank McIntire succeeded him in the presidency. C. D. Evans became cashier upon retirement of J. V. Curran in 1907, who at the time assumed the duties of county treasurer. It was in January, 1910, that the bank received its charter from the state as a savings institution. It began with a capital of $50,000.

Early history of South Ottumwa Savings Bank, from *History of Wapello County, Iowa,* by Harrison J. Waterman (published in 1914 by S. J. Clarke Publishing Co., Chicago).

The farm department would make calls in their suits to cattle feed lots and hog confinements. When they came back to the bank, no one had to ask where they'd been.

--Lowell McCracken

An old notary seal found in the bank's vault.

Examining Committee's Report to the Auditor of State of the Condition of

The South Ottumwa Savings Bank located at Ottumwa in the county of Wapello and State of Iowa, showing the condition at the close of business on Dec 19, 1912, as provided by Section 1871 of the Code as amended by Chapter 80, Acts of the Thirty-first General Assembly.

Examined Dec 20, 1912

Assets	Dollars Cts.	Liabilities	Dollars Cts.
Bills Receivable	365303 74	Capital Stock	50000
U. S. Bonds Hawaiian	5000	Individual Deposits subject to check	128094 02
Other Bonds		Demand Certificates	
Municipal Warrants		Time Certificates	37361 11
Cash	8662 12	Savings Deposits	260202 22
Cash Items	5012 49	Bank Deposits	
Due from Banks	119452 93	Bills Payable Postal Savi.	681 24
Overdrafts	1621 96	Re-discounts	
Bank Building and Lot		Bank Overdrafts	
Other Real Estate		Unpaid Dividends	
Furniture and Fixtures	1277 47	Surplus	15000
Expenses		Undivided Profits	14493 02
Other Assets		Due Clearing House	
Total	506330 61	Total	506330 61

BONDS OF OFFICERS

Are the officers or employes bonded?

If so, give title of such officers and employes and amount of bond required of each

Cashier $5000.00

Kind of bond Personal

A four-page report to the auditor of the State of Iowa, detailing the financial position of the South Ottumwa Savings Bank as of the close of business on December 20, 1912. The bank reported total assets of just over a half-million dollars, including "furniture and fixtures" worth $1,277.47. Individual deposit checking accounts totaled $128,094.02.

OFFICERS AND DIRECTORS

Names	Overdrafts	Liability to Bank: As Borrower	Liability to Bank: As Endorser
Arbenz, Paul		600.00	
Dain, Joseph		4000.00	
Hand, B. A.		50.00	450.00
Wormhoudt, John	Farm loan	7000	606

Pres.

Vice-Pres.

Cashier

Ass. Cashier

What amount is loaned to corporations in which any of the directors are interested? Dain Mfg Co 5000.00

Have all loans to officers and directors been approved as per Section 1880 of the Code? Yes

In your opinion are all the notes in the bills receivable genuine? Yes

Have you made personal inspection of the same? Yes

In your opinion are all the notes in the bills receivable the actual property of the bank and not such as might be left for safe-keeping or collection? Yes

Does the bank preserve all cancelled drafts and certificates? Yes

Are they filed in numerical order? No. In order of payment

What amount of certificates of deposit represent money borrowed? None

Name of bank or person to whom issued

Amount of collateral attached

What rate of interest paid on above certificates?

What amount of bills receivable more than three months past due? 5625.00

Several of the bank directors were also listed as borrowers in the auditor's report, including Joseph Dain who had borrowed $4,000. His business, Dain Manufacturing, had taken out a loan of an additional $5,000. Past-due loans owed to the bank totaled $5,625.00.

South Ottumwa Savings Bank

List of doubtful paper which should be charged off:

NAMES OF BORROWERS	Dollars	Cts.
None		

List of doubtful paper which should be secured:

NAMES OF BORROWERS	Dollars	Cts.
None		

Loans exceeding the legal limit: (Overdrafts to be classed as loans.)

NAMES OF BORROWERS	Dollars	Cts.
None		

Has the management directed these loans to be reduced to the limit? ....

If not, why not? ....

Has the management directed the overdrafts to be taken up and practice discontinued? .... Yes ....

If not, why not? ....

What is the actual cash value of the banking house? ....

What is the actual cash value of furniture and fixtures? .... $1500.00 ....

The auditor seemed to feel the furniture and fixtures were more valuable than the bank management did, listing the value at $1,500. There was no "doubtful paper" and no troubled loans.

What amount of probable loss on real estate, other than banking property? None

What amount of bills payable are outstanding? None

What amount of re-discounts are outstanding? None

In making this report does the Examining Committee prove for itself all items included in this statement? Yes

Is this report made by an officer of the bank and signed by the Committee without an actual knowledge of the existing conditions? No

We the undersigned, the Examining Committee for the above bank, do solemnly swear the foregoing statement is true and correct according to our best knowledge and belief.

F. Von Shrader

B. A. Hand

Subscribed and sworn to before me by F. Von Shrader & B. A. Hand

this 21 day of Dec 1912

Ruby Rudd

Notary Public in and for

Wapello County, Iowa.

Note.—Section 1871 of the Code provides for quarterly examinations all of which are to be spread on the records of the bank. Copies of the June and December reports are to be filed with the Auditor of State.

Examining Committee's Report

To the Auditor of State

of the Condition of

South Ottumwa Savings Bank, Ottumwa, Iowa

At the close of business Dec 19 1912

Ruby Rudd, Notary Public in Wapello County, witnessed the signatures of F. Von Shrader and B. A. Hand on the 1912 Statement of Condition of the bank.

STATEMENT OF THE CONDITION OF THE

South Ottumwa Savings Bank

organized under the laws of Iowa, located at Ottumwa, county of Wapello, at the close of business on the 28th day of June, 1913, made to the auditor of state.

ASSETS

Amount of bills, bonds and other evidence of debt discounted or purchased, actually owned by this bank		$ 404,658.00
Gold in vault	$ 1,750.00	
Silver in vault	245.00	
Legal tender, national bank notes and subsidiary coin	8,056.35	
Drafts, checks and other cash items not dishonored	2,953.89	
Total gold, silver, legal tender, drafts and checks, etc., carried out		13 008.24
Amount subject to be drawn at sight on deposit with solvent banks		94,018.09
Overdrafts		674.87
Value of personal property		3,500.00
Total assets		$ 515,878.70

LIABILITIES

Amount of capital stock		$ 50,000.00
Amount of deposits subject to check	$131,653.15	
Amount of time deposits	38,998.17	
Amount savings deposits	259,517.00	
Postal savings deposits	470.86	
Total deposits		430,639.1[illegible]
Surplus fund		15,000.00
Other profits after deducting expenses		20,[illegible]9.52
Total liabilities		$ 515,878.70

State of Iowa, Wapello county, ss:

We, Frank McIntire, president and C. D. Evans, cashier, of bank above named, do solemnly swear that the foregoing statement is full, true and correct, to the best of our knowledge and belief, and that the assets therein set forth are bona fide the property of said bank in its corporate capacity, and that no part of the same has been loaned or advanced to said bank for the purpose of being exhibited as a portion of its assets.

FRANK M'INTIRE, President.
C. D. EVANS, Cashier.

Sworn to before me and subscribed in my presence by Frank McIntire and C. D. Evans this 5th day of July, 1913.

C. L. M'MINN, Notary Public in and for Wapello county.

Attested by: F. VON SCHRADER.
B. P. BROWN
Directors.

Statement of the Bank's condition on June 28, 1913.

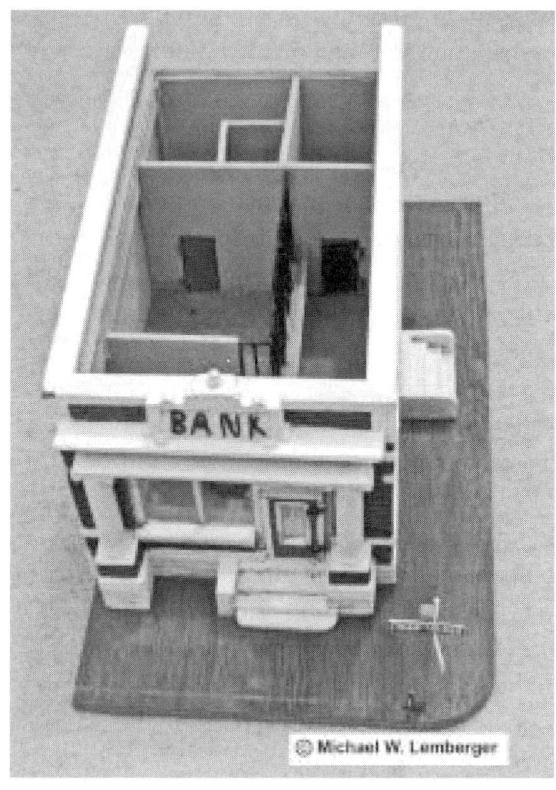

Model of the original 1912 South Ottumwa Savings Bank building. This model shows the building as it existed around 1935, when electricity and plumbing were added. The model was created by Mr. Glen Eakins. Until recently the model was exhibited at the Wapello County Historical Society Museum; it is now on permanent display at the Main Bank.

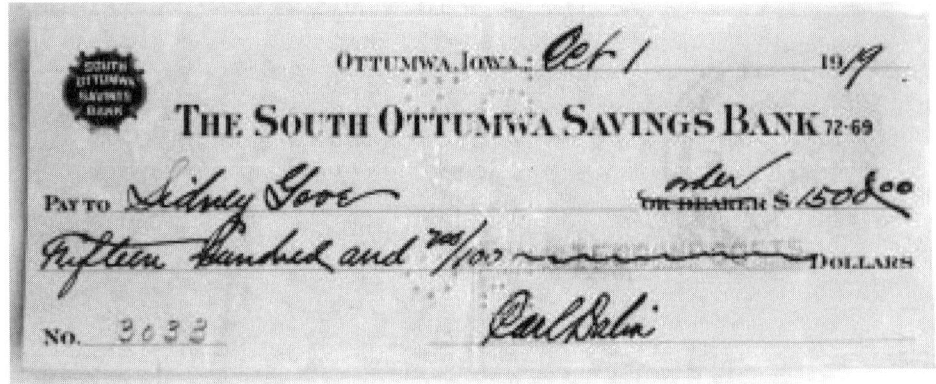
OTTUMWA, IOWA, Oct 1 1919

THE SOUTH OTTUMWA SAVINGS BANK 72-69

PAY TO Sidney Goore order ~~OR BEARER~~ $1500.00

Fifteen Hundred and 00/100 DOLLARS

NO. 3033

South Ottumwa Savings Bank check for $1,500 written October 1, 1919. The number at bottom left is the customer's savings account number. The dots at center are holes punched during the clearing process, showing that the check has been paid.

A lot has happened between the 1970s and 2014. Customers are using more electronic banking, internet banking, and banking from their smart phones. But there was a time when all that wasn't even a thought. The bank lobby was always full and the teller line was always busy.

Our head teller, Margie Tennyson, was in command of the "ship" and did a tremendous job. Everything was done by hand and computers were only just informational banking terminals. We would close the lobby at 2:00 p.m. and balance our windows, which was a task in itself – but at the time it was just the norm. We would add up pennies, nickels, dimes, etc., then add in our pinks (cash in) and whites (cash out). After getting individual totals, we added every other window's totals and finally reached the grand total. There was no bill counter, and our change counter had to be turned by hand.

--Kathy Ebelsheisher

Those of us who were here in the 1970s have seen a lot of changes. This was long before the age of technology. We ran the teller line with an adding machine and spindles.

These were the days when everyone's Social Security was paid on the 3rd of each month. On this date the bank lobby would be completely filled with customers from the time we opened until the bank closed. The lines seemed endless. During these busy times it was not uncommon to see Bob Ackley, bank president, and Don Roemerman, executive vice president, along with other senior management, helping customers by working between teller windows.

-- Nancy McWilliams

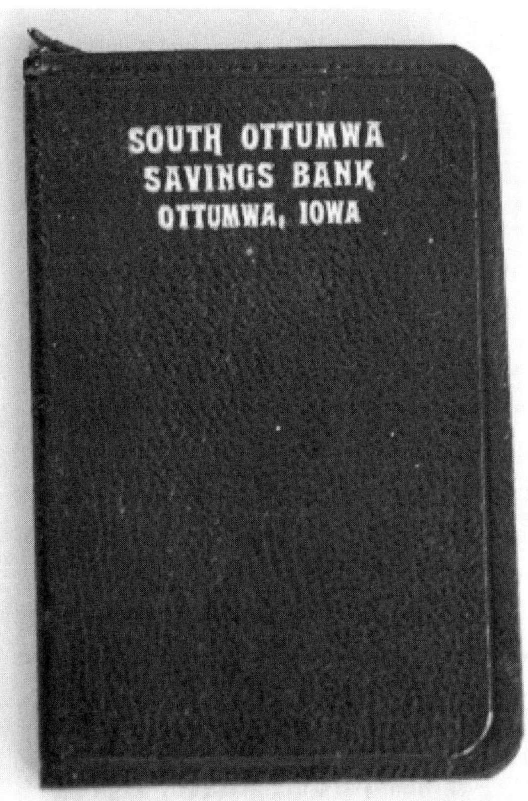

This savings account passbook from 1924 is shown close to actual size -- 2.5 by 3.5 inches. Records of deposits and withdrawals were made by hand.

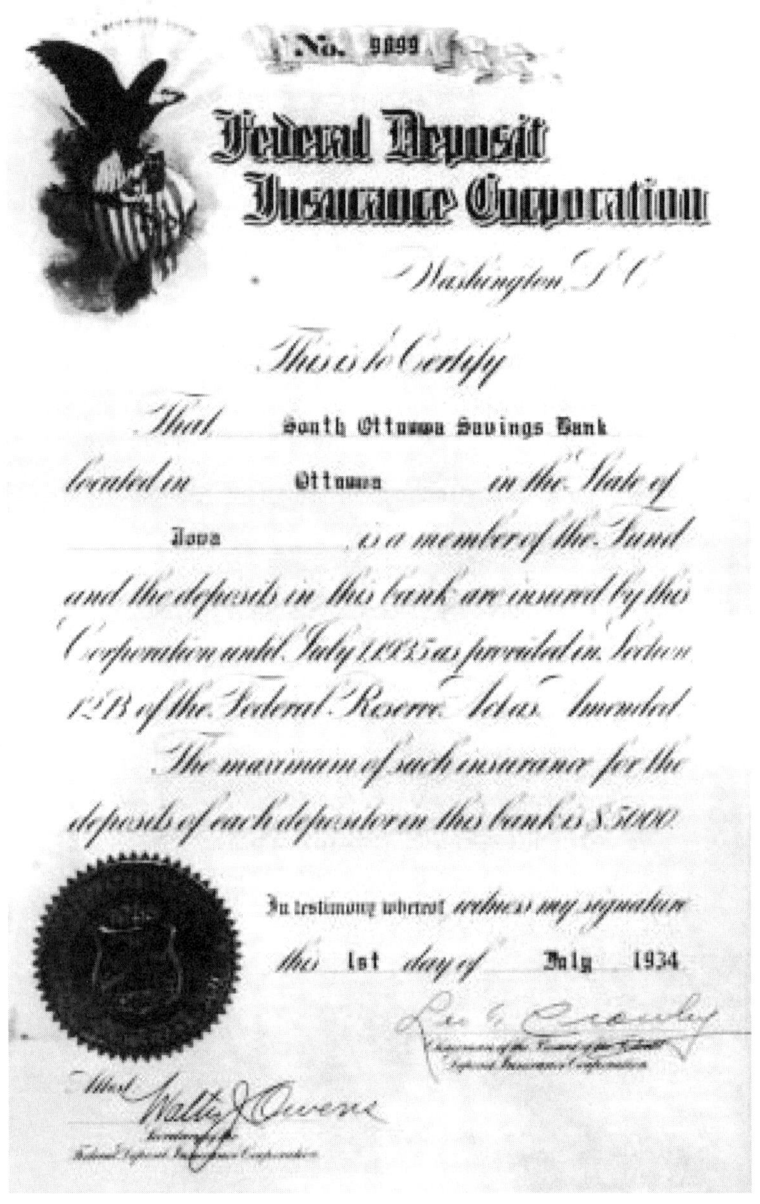

No. 9899

Federal Deposit Insurance Corporation

Washington D.C.

This is to Certify

That South Ottumwa Savings Bank located in Ottumwa in the State of Iowa is a member of the Fund and the deposits in this bank are insured by this Corporation until July 1 1935 as provided in Section 12B of the Federal Reserve Act as amended.

The maximum of such insurance for the deposits of each depositor in this bank is $5000.

In testimony whereof witness my signature this 1st day of July 1934

Leo T. Crowley
Chairman of the Board of the Federal Deposit Insurance Corporation

Attest Walter J. Owens
Secretary of the Federal Deposit Insurance Corporation

After the stock market crash of 1929 and the Great Depression led to hundreds of bank failures, the federal government established the Federal Deposit Insurance Corporation (FDIC) in 1933 to help restore customer confidence, insuring accounts up to $2,500. By 1934, South Ottumwa Savings Bank was a member of the FDIC, and insurance per depositor had increased to $5,000.

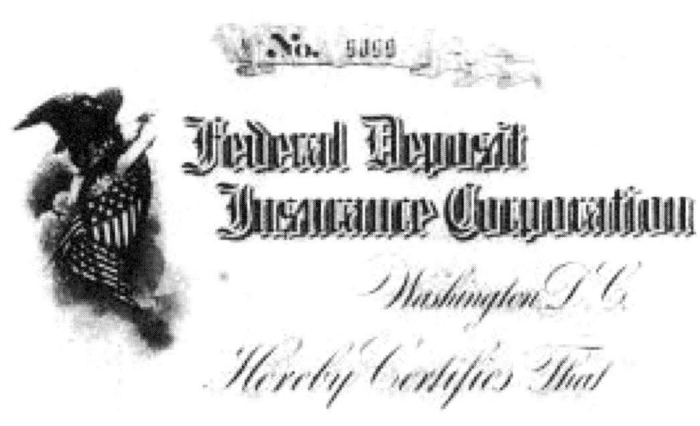

Federal Deposit Insurance Corporation

Washington D.C.

Hereby Certifies That

South Ottumwa Savings Bank

located in Ottumwa

in the State of Iowa

is an insured bank under the permanent plan for the insurance of deposits by the Federal Deposit Insurance Corporation, with maximum insurance of $5000 for each depositor as provided by Act of Congress.

In testimony whereof, witness my signature and the seal of the Corporation this 23rd day of August 1935

Leo T. Crowley
Chairman of the Board of Directors

Attest
Acting Secretary

The FDIC was originally enacted as a temporary measure. After the Banking Act of 1935 made the FDIC a permanent agency of the government, new certificates were issued to participating banks. The amount of insurance per depositor, set by the original act at $2,500, has grown to $250,000 as of 2008.

South Ottumwa Savings Bank, probably during the 1940s. Note that the awnings have disappeared in favor of distinctive white window treatments, and the front window consists of two panels rather than the single pane which appears in the photo on page 16. This building was replaced by a newer bank in 1964, and was demolished after the new bank opened. The new building occupied the site of the Do Drop Inn, visible at the left side of this photo.

Loan papers were typed manually on typewriters until in the early 1990s when the bank purchased loan processing software and Joan and Penny went to school to learn to use it.

Everyone in the loan department should remember the "bus" that was moved to and from the loan department with the work every day.

— Penny Reed

Looking southwest over South Ottumwa, 1940s. The Jefferson Street Viaduct is at left, with Victory Park located in the triangle formed by the street's split at the south end of the bridge. Church Street runs from center top to lower right, with the original river channel at right. The Coliseum is at lower right. South Ottumwa Savings Bank is barely visible just to the left of Church Street and just under the large white building near the top of the photo.

Tammy was the ATM for the bank, located in the front lobby. The commercial started out "Tammy, she's our personal banker..." What a song!

--Penny Reed

Church Street in the 1940s, looking toward the river. The buildings at right occupy the site which later became Fareway grocery and in 2014 the new addition to South Ottumwa Savings Bank. Just beyond the buildings is the southern end of the Jefferson Street Viaduct. The smokestacks are those of the Iowa Southern Utilities power generating plant located between Green and Jefferson Streets, on the northern bank of the river.

Hard to believe, but in 1989 we didn't have computers in the bank. I convinced the president that we could save time and manpower if he would get one. He finally agreed, and the only problem was that none of management or employees really knew how to operate it. I called my daughter, a college student, who came home one weekend and showed us how to make spreadsheets on Lotus. All the departments would take turns using the computer for their work, and we fought for time for each of us to get our work done.

Amazing when you consider every person has one now.

—Gail Bainbridge

On our real busy days, like the first of the month, we got a lot of help from upper management. Bob Ackley, bank president, would always make sure we "girls" had plenty of energy to get through those busy first-of-the-month days, with pizza for everyone. We would open the front doors of the bank just so the lines could stretch out. This was such a busy time, and it was tiring. By the end of the day, however, it wasn't so bad – and looking back now, there are memories I will always cherish.

--Kathy Ebelsheisher

1940s view of the Des Moines River, showing the original layout of the river channels, with the main channel looping off to the left. Note the original small hydro dam, near center, and the Y-shaped southern end of the Jefferson Street Viaduct, at lower left. The original Market Street Bridge is at center, with the Ottumwa Coliseum / Armory on the left bank of the river.

South Ottumwa Savings Bank

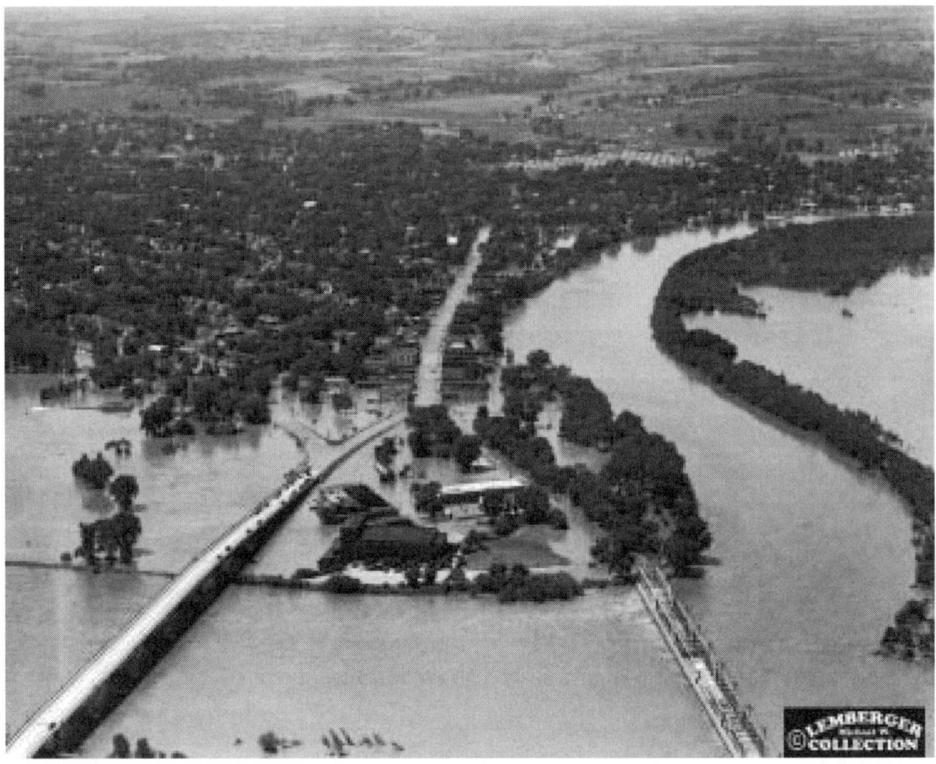

Flood of 1947 showing South Ottumwa. The Jefferson Street Viaduct is at lower left and Market Street Bridge at lower right, with Church Street running through the center of the photo. Central Addition is at right, under water. The Coliseum stands on the riverbank between the bridges, surrounded by flood water. The original river channel -- which became the lagoons in Ottumwa Park after the river straightening project of the 1950s and 1960s -- sweeps through South Ottumwa at right, bending to flow under the bridges. South Ottumwa Savings Bank is barely visible at the center of the photo.

It was not uncommon to "pop" when balancing at the end of the day. This meant that when the teller balanced their drawer, it was correct to the penny the first time through. Apparently busy times kept us focused on both the customer and the accuracy of teller services.

--Nancy McWilliams

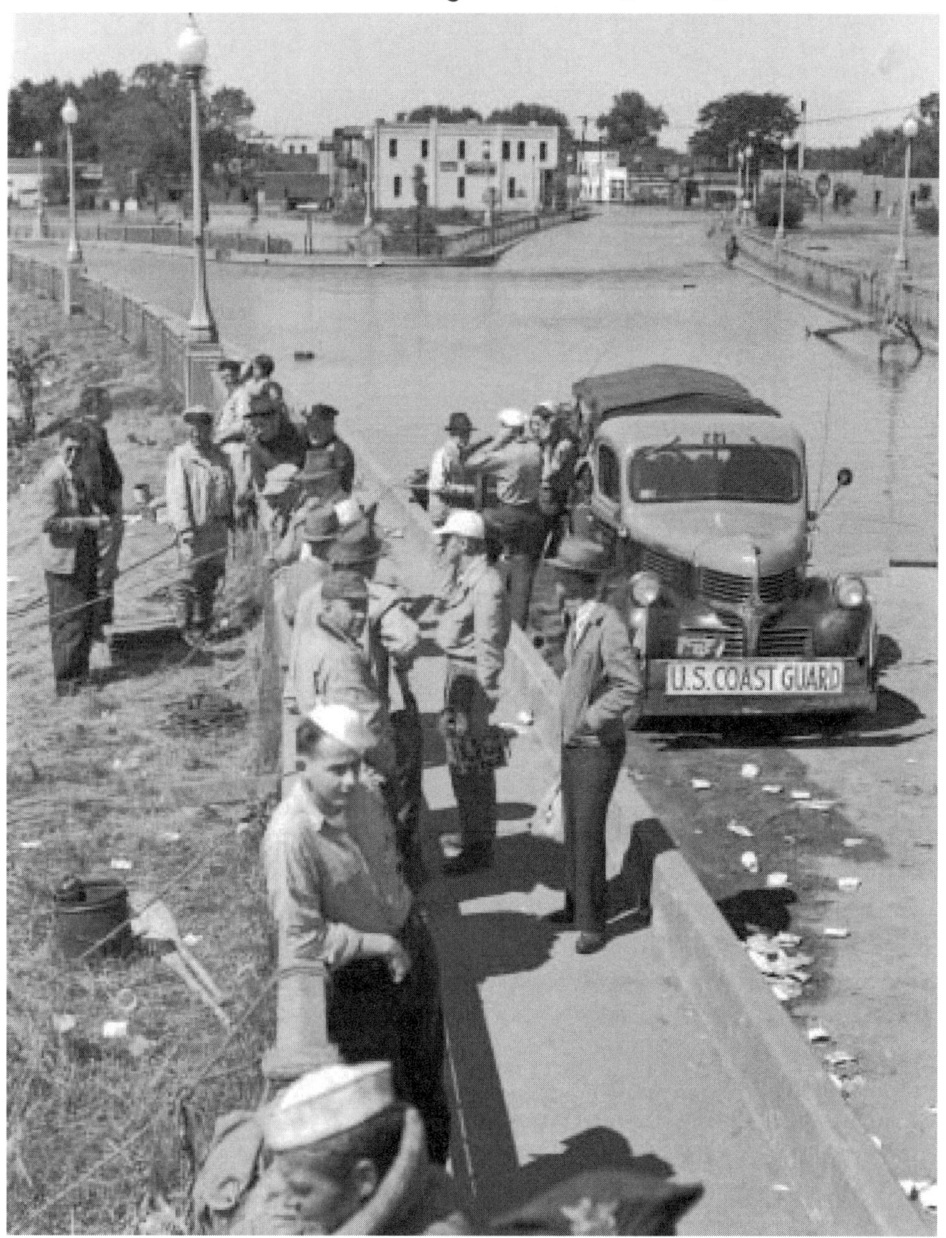

During the 1947 floods, Naval and Coast Guard personnel stationed at Naval Air Station Ottumwa pitched in to help wherever needed. Sailors and civilian personnel work at the flooded south end of the Jefferson Street Viaduct. The buildings at top center were removed to build Fareway, which in turn was removed to build the 2014 addition to South Ottumwa Savings Bank.

South Ottumwa Savings Bank

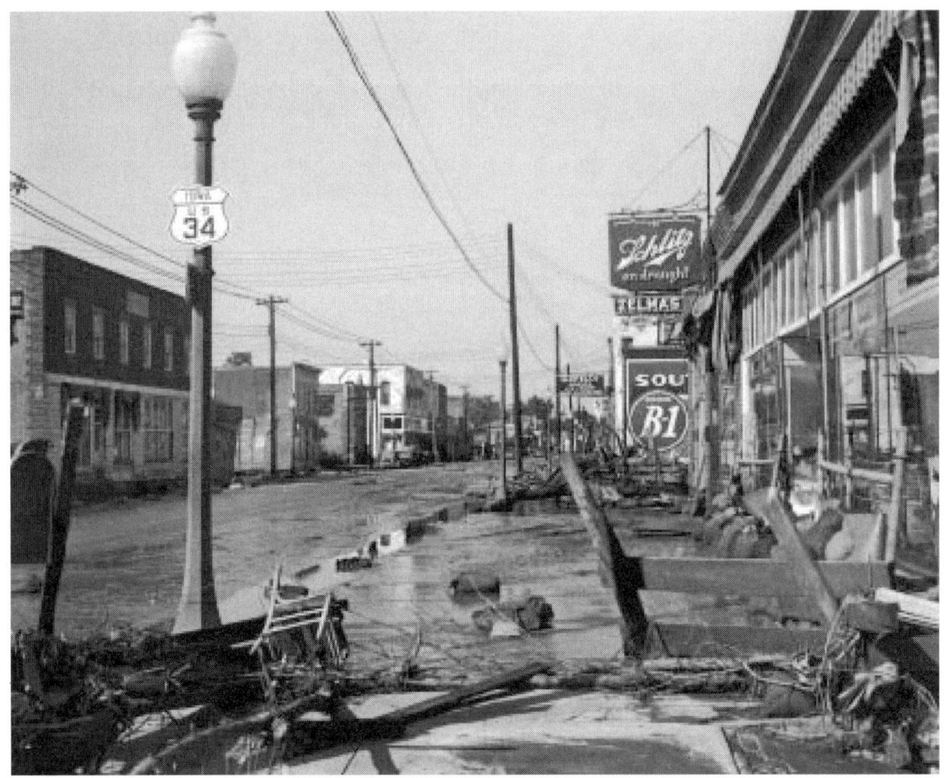

Flood of 1947, showing debris and standing water on Church Street. This view was taken from Myrtle Street looking toward Five Corners. South Ottumwa Savings Bank, with its distinctive peaked facade, is visible just left of center.

South Ottumwa Savings Bank helped to start the first Southeast Iowa Farm Safety Just 4 Kids Program. Lowell McCracken and Penny Reed held the first Farm Safety Just 4 Kids Safety Camp with over 100 participants. It's now a nationally-known program, which we're proud to be part of.

South Ottumwa Savings Bank could be seen at the Wapello County Fair with a booth promoting their products. What fun! We raffled small pedal tractors. People enjoyed seeing the employees in Eldon!

— Penny Reed

The lobby of the bank had a wood-burning fireplace, and at Christmas time we always had a huge real Christmas tree. The South Ottumwa Boosters always had a Sunday Open House to kick off the Christmas season. Mr. and Mrs. Santa Claus were in the lobby for the kids to visit and receive candy. Employees baked cookies and we passed them out to everyone who came. We opened Christmas Club accounts and gave away pie plates to everyone that opened an account. We also gave out our calendars for the New Year. It was always a huge event. — Sue Shannon

---

Damage caused by the 1947 floods. This photo was taken on Church Street near Riverside Park. The white building at right center stands on the site of the South Ottumwa Saving Bank's 2014 addition. The service station and house to the left of Church Street are now the site of Bridge View Center's parking lot.

The daily transactions were bundled at the end of day and sent by carrier to our correspondent bank in Des Moines for posting. Checks drawn on SOSB were returned the next morning. Employees filed these in customer bins, checking each signature, amount, and date. Statements were done by hand, and the checks were returned to the customer.

— Nancy McWilliams

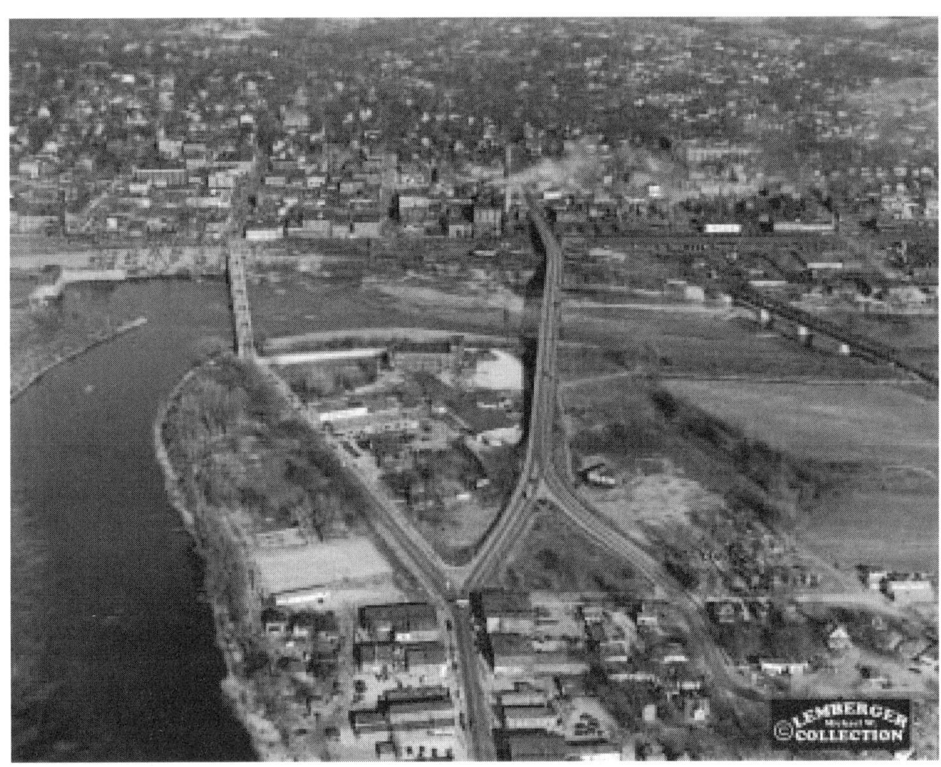

Looking north toward the river and downtown in about 1950, before the river straightening project was begun. The original hydro dam is at center left. The Market Street Bridge and Jefferson Street Viaduct are at top, with the Ottumwa Colisem on the riverbank between the two. The railroad bridge (now the walking trail) is at right. The earliest South Ottumwa Savings Bank, with its distinctive white arched windows, is at lower center. The Do Drop Inn -- a repurposed Quonset hut from World War II -- is just above the bank in this view.

South Ottumwa Savings Bank after a 1955 remodeling. This is the same building pictured on pages 16 and 28. The windows along the side of the building, barely visible in this image, remained, but the front of the building was entirely changed.

Our first ATM was a joy! Twenties went in one drawer, fives in another. There were no sensors to assure the drawers were put in right, so sometimes a customer would ask for $100 and get five $5 bills instead of five $20 bills. You can be sure the customers complained.

—Gail Bainbridge

Church and Weller Streets, 1950s. In this night shot, South Ottumwa Savings Bank is among the buildings at left.

Church Street in the 1950s, showing traffic coming from Market Street at left and Jefferson Street at center. The Main Bank's 2014 addition occupies the site of the buildings at right.

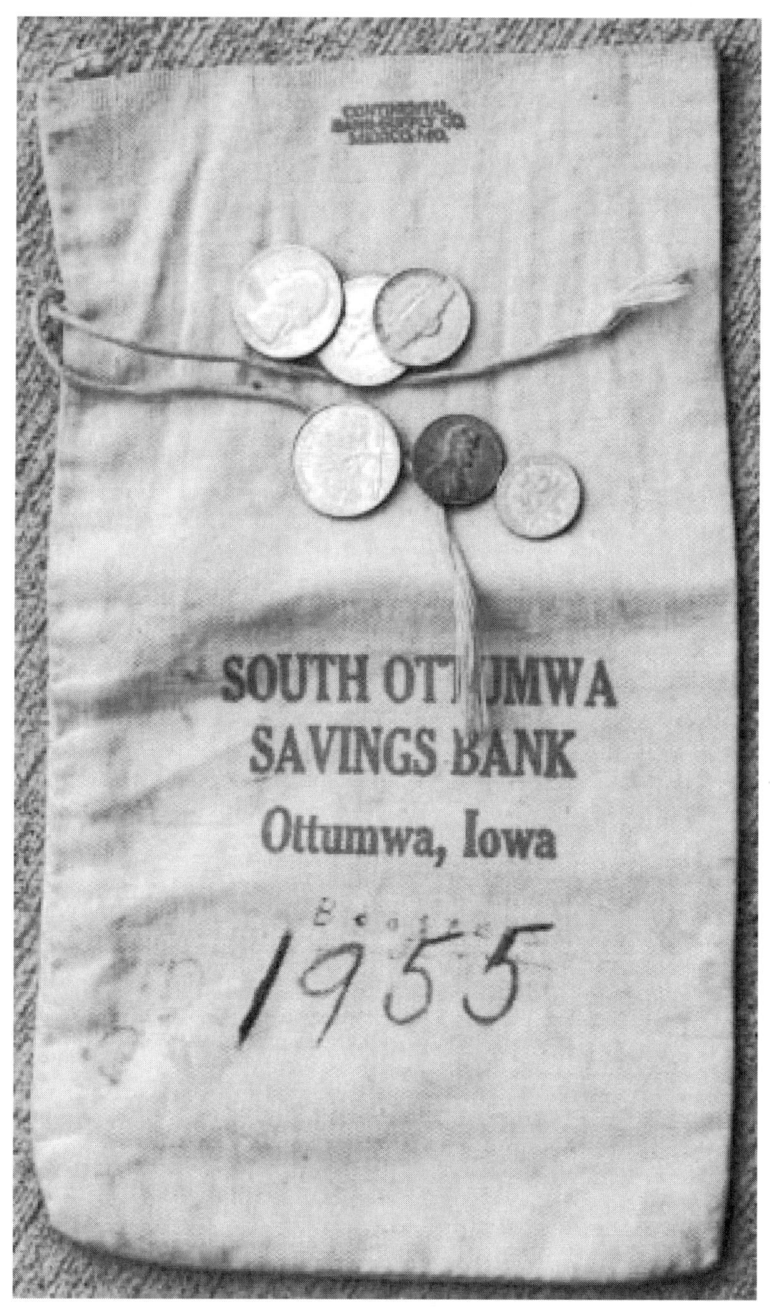

A coin sack from 1955.

I started working at SOSB in 1985 as a teller. We were a full service bank on Saturdays, which was considered a business day. We didn't have an automated teller system, but instead used a calculator, two spindles (one for cash out and one for cash in) and a balancing sheet to balance our window each day. The bookkeeping department still had an old fashioned proof machine and a posting machine.

— Sue Shannon

DIRECTORS

Myron L. Ackley
President

Harold Anderson
South Side Drug

Guy Day
Refrigeration &
Air Conditioning

H. H. Evans
Cashier

C. Lee Kapp
General Insurance

Mrs. R. L. Pollard

Ernest Schoech
Farmer

Ralph Watson
Assistant Cashier

OFFICERS

Myron L. Ackley .... President
H. H. Evans .... Vice President and Cashier
Ralph Watson .... Assistant Cashier
Robert K. Ackley .... Assistant Cashier

SOUTH

OTTUMWA

SAVINGS BANK

OTTUMWA, IOWA

This small pamphlet is a statement of the condition of South Ottumwa Savings Bank as of December 31, 1956, with the directors and officers listed on the back.

Additions were built to the bank, and then a new motor bank was completed. My, what a success that was! Working on day one was quite a challenge. There were cars backed up towards Ace Hardware as if the bank was giving away free money. There were five drive-up lanes and three very busy gals inside. It was quite fun sending tubes in and out. What a convenient way to do your banking without getting out of your car – and what a time those first few months were.

—Kathy Ebelsheisher

SOUTH OTTUMWA SAVINGS BANK

OTTUMWA, IOWA

STATEMENT OF CONDITION DECEMBER 31, 1956

ASSETS

Cash on hand and on deposit with banks		$ 884,500.93
United States Government Securities		1,875,818.00
Other Bonds and Securities		40,150.25
Loans and Discounts		1,264,871.07
Bank Building		38,141.28
Furniture and Fixtures		12,550.39
		$4,034,828.84

LIABILITIES

Deposits		$3,778,348.46
Capital	100,000.00	
Surplus	100,000.00	
Undivided Profits	56,478.38	256,478.38
		$4,034,828.84

Member of Federal Deposit Insurance Corporation

The interior of the pamphlet lists assets and liabilities as of December 31, 1956.

(1956 Ad)

HAVE YOU PLANNED FOR YOUR FUTURE?

Money saved regularly is the key to independence and security for your future. Open a savings account here, watch it grow at our high bank interest into a worry-free future for you!

South Ottumwa Savings Bank

MEMBER OF FEDERAL DEPOSIT INSURANCE CORP.

See us for ALL Banking Needs

We were all working late as we had just bought Peoples Savings and Loan. Lowell went upstairs – I don't know why; ask Mike Miller.

I was working in the back room when I heard the crash. I thought someone fell down the stairs – we were all tired and carrying things back and forth from the Peoples location.

Lowell had fallen through the ceiling and landed in front of the copy machine looking like the Abominable Snowman. All covered in insulation, with electric wires hanging everywhere.

After we were sure he was okay, we all laughed at the sight of him. That year at the Christmas party we paid tribute to Lowell with a song – *Up On the Rooftop*, revised to commemorate the occasion.

—Gail Bainbridge

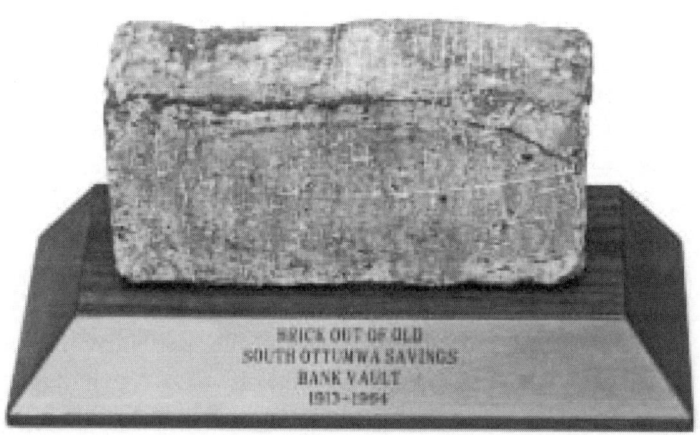

© Michael W. Lemberger

Souvenir brick from the vault in the original South Ottumwa Saving Bank building at the corner of Church and Weller. The building, built in 1912, was torn down in 1964 after a larger facility was constructed next door.

South Ottumwa Savings Bank

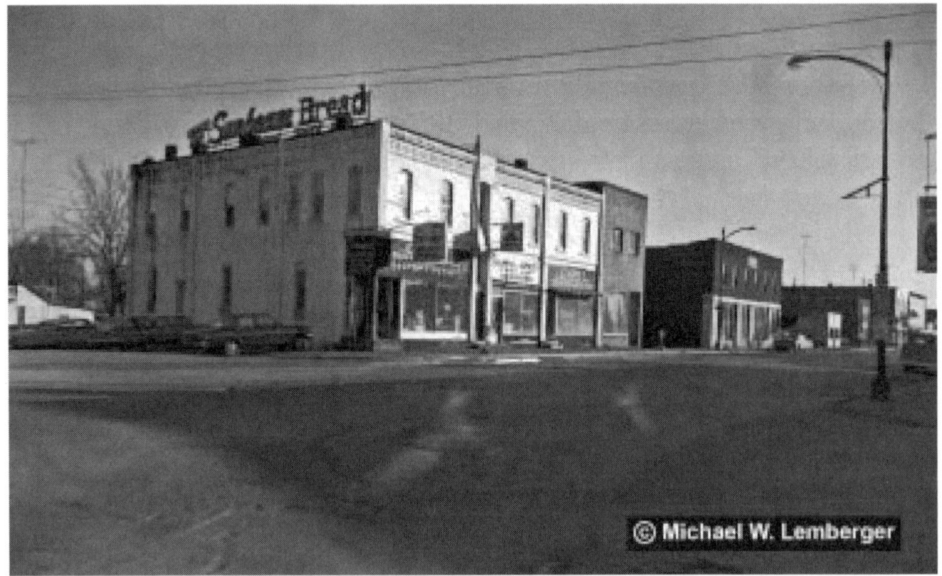

Church Street from Myrtle Street, March 1963. Most of the buildings in this photo were removed to build the Fareway grocery store which occupied the site until 2008, when the building was purchased by South Ottumwa Savings Bank and demolished. The bank's 2014 addition now occupies this site. The original bank building is barely visible just to the left of the speed limit sign.

As a whole staff, we worked well together – we made it not only a good place to work but an enjoyable one. We celebrated birthdays (cake, of course), had a Christmas party each year, and best of all was waiting for "bonus time".

We also had our busy time – first of every month, Social Security time. It was before payments came to the bank. Customers would line up at the door before 9:00 a.m. which was opening time and be ready to come in the door. It would be a continual line until almost closing. All has changed now with all the computers, etc. It was then I decided it was time to retire and enjoy life with my family, but I'm happy to say I enjoyed working at South Ottumwa Savings Bank.

—Margie Tennyson

Christmas time was always fun. Our fireplace in the lobby always fascinated the little ones. We decorated the fireplace for Santa, and our youngest customers would look up inside as if Santa was on his way down. The South Side merchants would always have a Sunday open house, and the bank would be decorated in Christmas colors with a large tree and refreshments of cookies and punch. Mr. & Mrs. Claus would sit in front of the fireplace greeting the kids and listening to their wishes for an awesome Christmas present.

Christmas wasn't the only time the bank was decorated. Crazy Days was always a fun time. All of the employees dressed for the occasion as the merchants had all their merchandise on the sidewalks. There are so many memories – funny how fast time goes, and how things change.

— Kathy Ebelsheisher

This 1963 view shows demolition underway, clearing the 300 block of Church Street so the Fareway grocery store could be built. This is the site of the 2014 addition to the main South Ottumwa Savings Bank building.

After a new building was completed in 1964, the original 1912 building was removed. In this view, the vault and front facade are still in place as demolition proceeds.

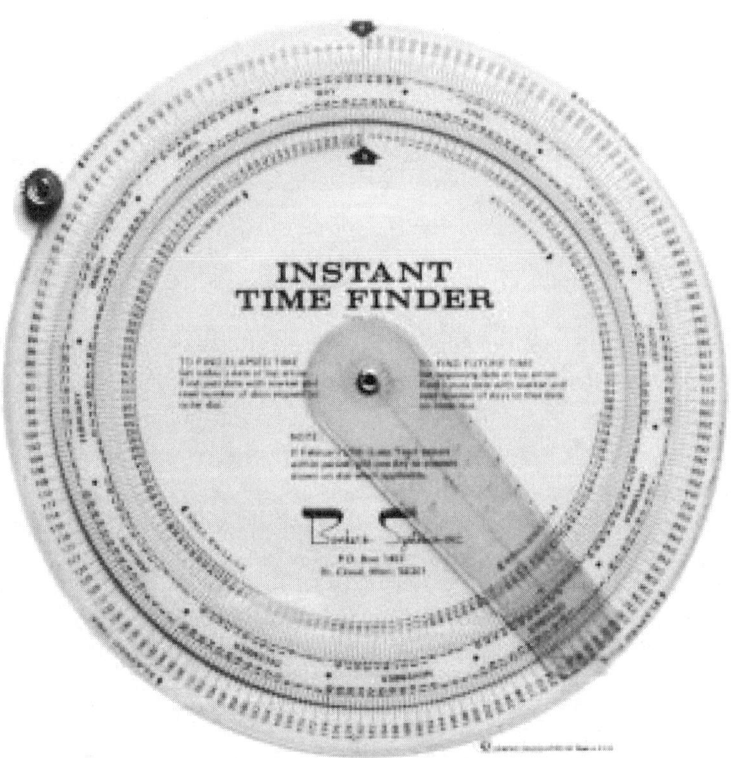

The instant time finder allowed a loan officer to determine exactly how many days had passed since a loan was issued or a payment was made, or how many days remained until the loan or the next payment was due.

Postcard view of the South Ottumwa Savings Bank building which opened in 1964.

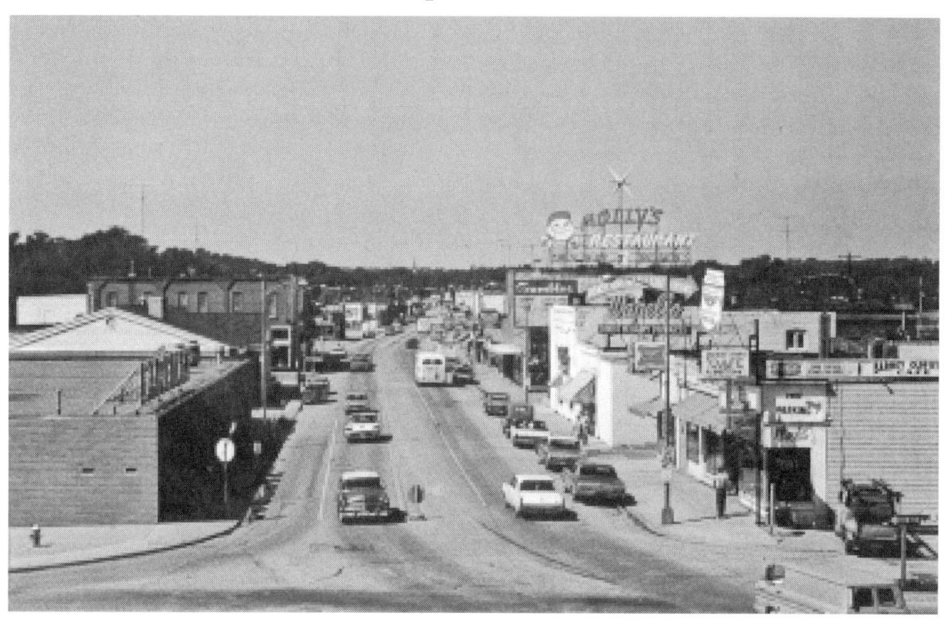

View of Church Street from the highway 34/63 overpass about 1965. At left is Fareway grocery store, on the site of the 2014 expansion of South Ottumwa Savings Bank. Just beyond Fareway, the peaked roof of the 1964 bank building is visible.

South Ottumwa Savings Bank

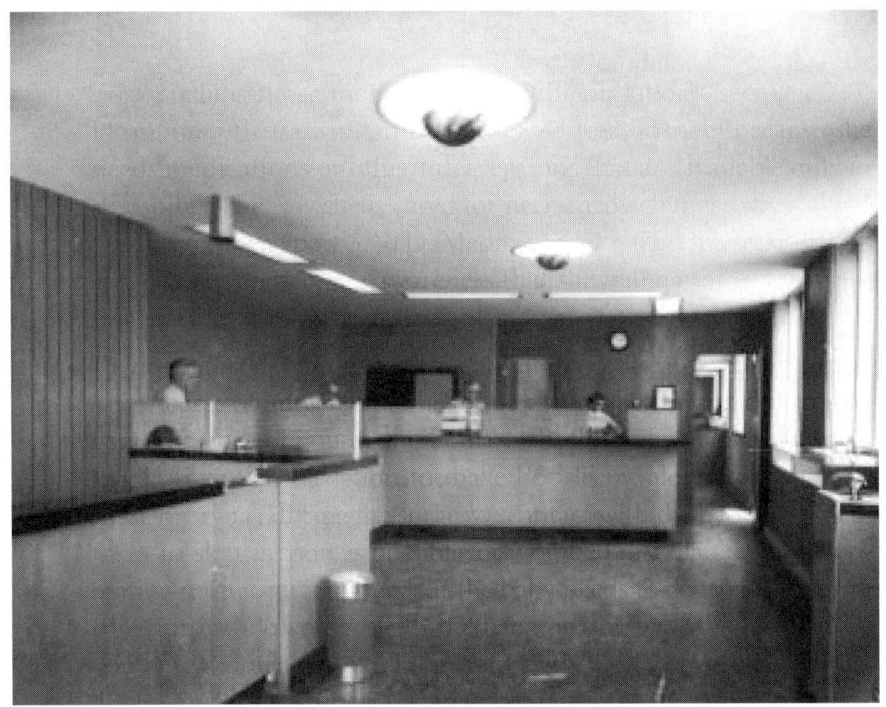

South Ottumwa Savings Bank lobby in the 1960s.

Myron Ackley

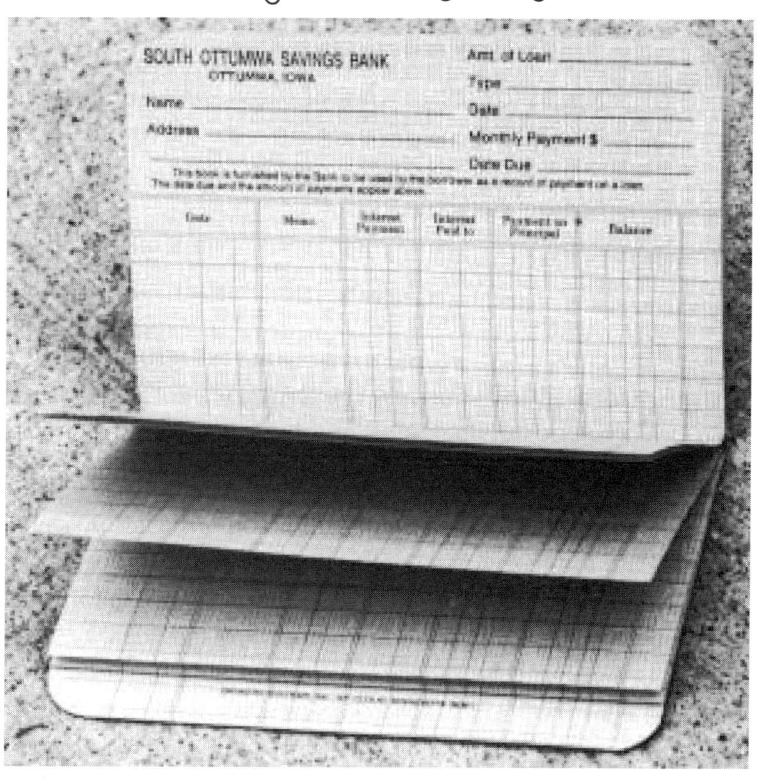

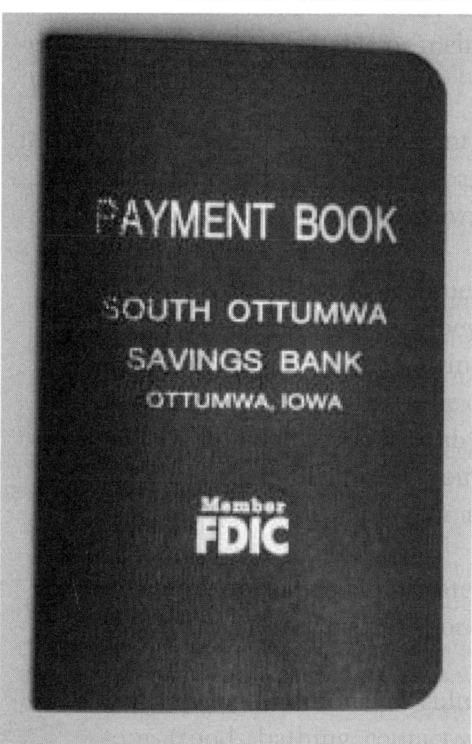

Payment book used by the loan department at South Ottumwa Savings Bank. The customer presented the book with each installment, and payments and balances were recorded by hand.

Bob Ackley (*at left*)

Ralph Watson was the cashier of the bank and farm loan officer. He would wear a carpenter's apron at farm sales so he could take payments as he was clerking. When he retired the bank bought him an electric riding lawn mower, which we rode right up to the table in the Ottumwa Country Club.

What a great person and teacher!

-- Lowell McCracken

Myron Ackley *(at left)*

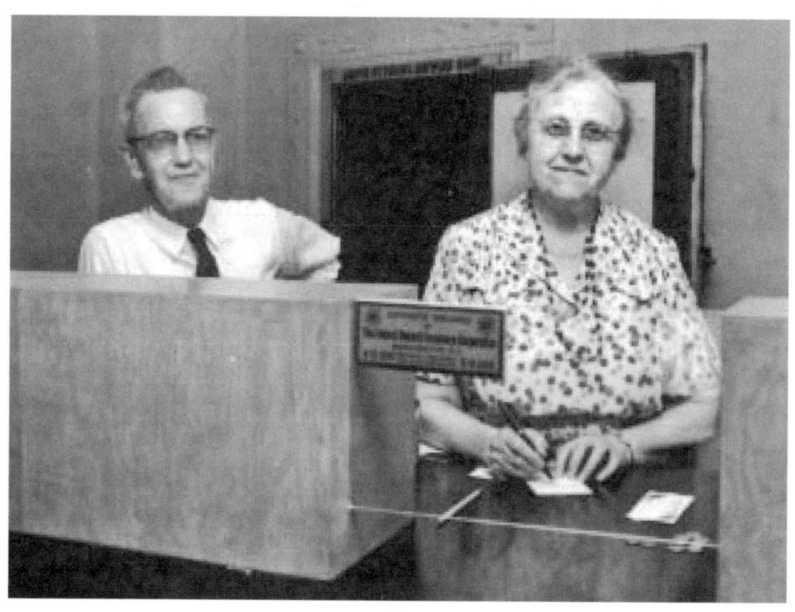

Ralph Watson (*at left*)

The vault door from the first bank building was saved when the building was demolished. It was installed in the Main Bank built in1964, where it continues to serve as the door of a storage room.

The inside of the old vault door, showing the storage room.

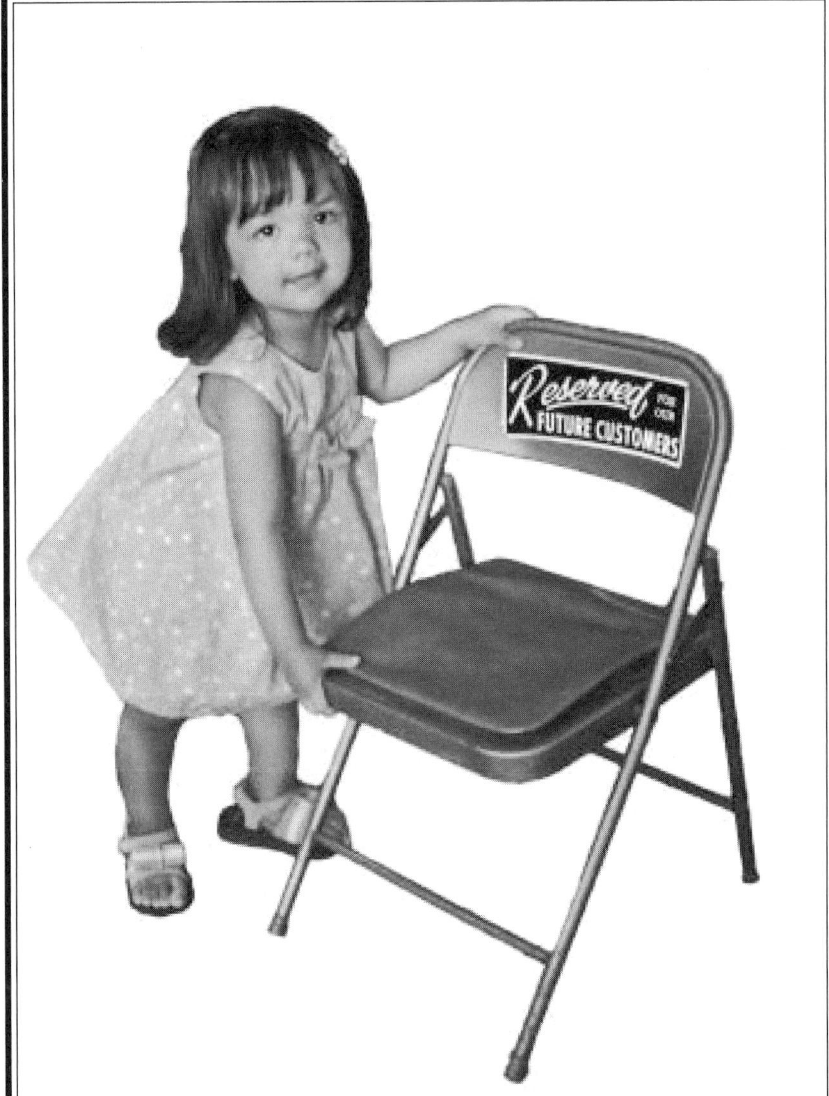

photo by Michael W. Lemberger

Alexis Henderson, 18-month-old daughter of Travis and Dr. Florita Henderson of Ottumwa, enjoys a chair which was used in the 1970s by children visiting the bank's lobby. One of a set, the chair was "reserved for our future customers."

HALF-CENTURY — Mrs. Ralph E. Watson helps her husband celebrate his 50th anniversary of work with the South Ottumwa Savings Bank Tuesday. He started work Feb. 1, 1922, and is now vice-president and cashier. Not only is Watson well-known in banking but also as a clerk for farm sales. Watson is not retiring. He was presented a watch and cake for his 50 years of service (Courier photo.)

Ottumwa *Courier*, 1972

I started out in the loan department and we all worked out of one money drawer – and we usually balanced to the penny. We took loan payments and recorded them on paper ledger sheets. Every loan had its own ledger sheet. We had tickler cards for all customers, which kept track of their loan history. We always had crispies or cinnamon rolls to eat. On Saturdays we had to stay until the whole bank was balanced.

—Rae Albertson

Artist's sketch of the South Ottumwa Savings Bank at the intersection of Pennsylvania and Elm. The branch opened in 1976, marking the first time SOSB had an office on the north side of the Des Moines River. The Penn-Elm Bank closed in the summer of 2011.

Part savings bank and part toy, this colorful car appealed to children of all ages.

Giveaways enjoyed
by customers
through the years

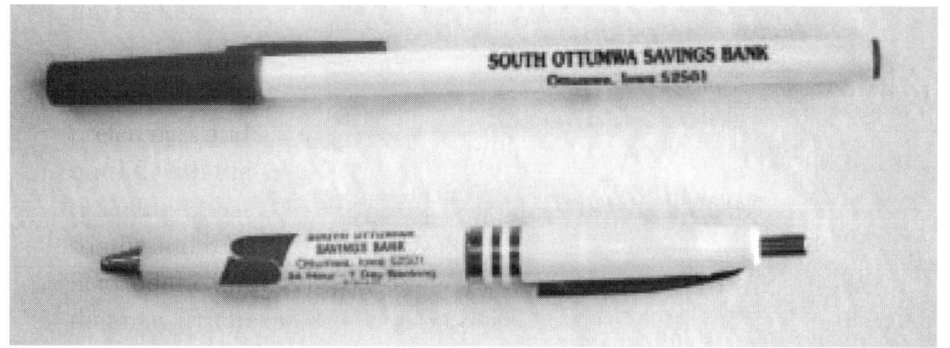

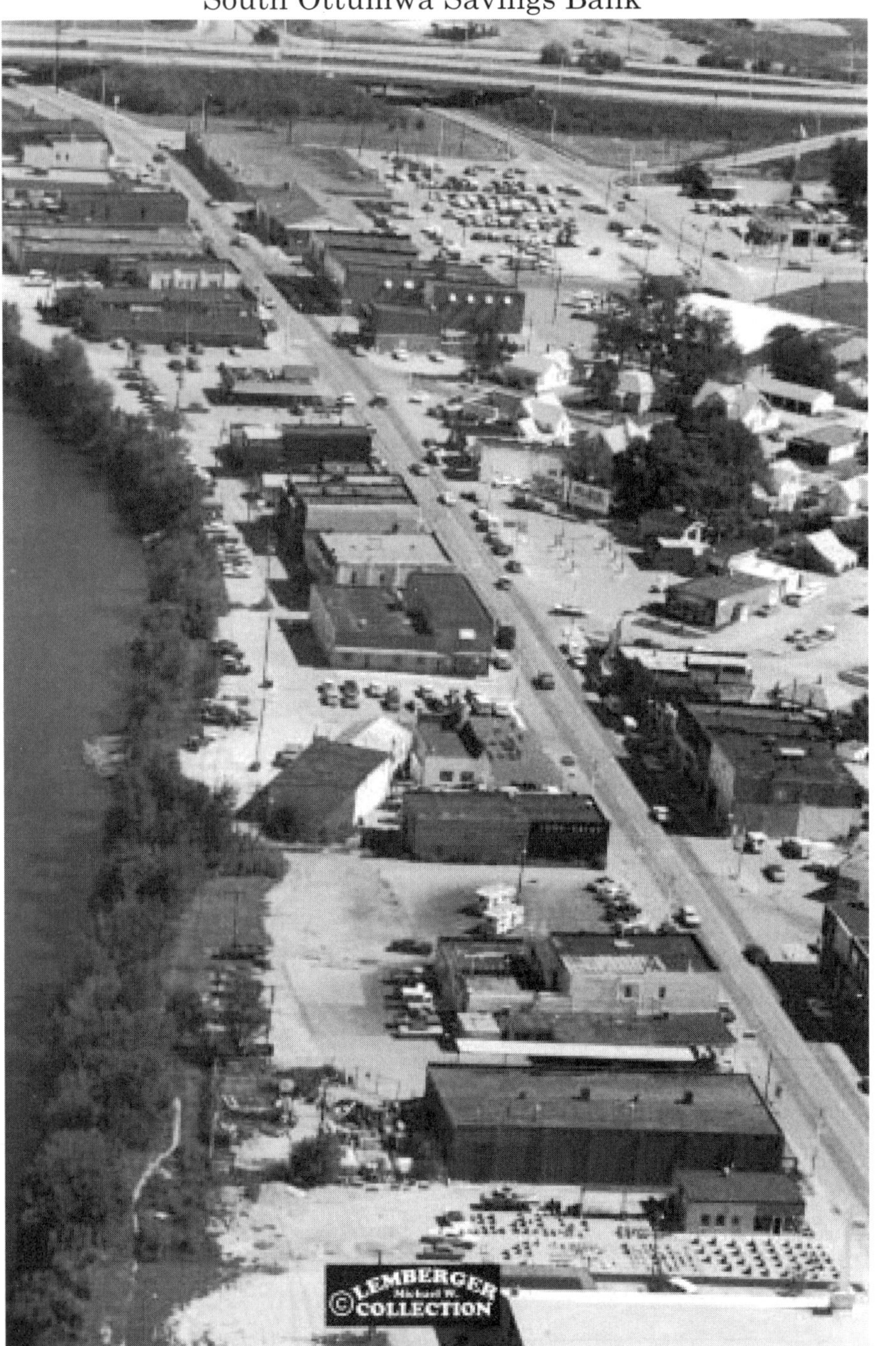

Church Street in 1978, looking northeast toward the river and downtown. The South Ottumwa Savings Bank built in the 1960s is near the top of the photo. Fareway grocery store is between the bank building and Highway 34 and 63 (top of photo). One of the Ottumwa Park lagoons is at left.

Grand Opening

Friday and Saturday, September 12th & 13th

Friday 9 to 5:30 Saturday 8 to 12

SOUTH OTTUMWA SAVINGS BANK HAS A BRAND NEW MOTOR BANK

South Ottumwa Savings Bank invites all it's customers in Ottumwa and surrounding area to drive thru and help us celebrate the Grand Opening of our new drive-up motor bank at 501 N. Weller St., 1 block South of our main office, across from the YMCA.

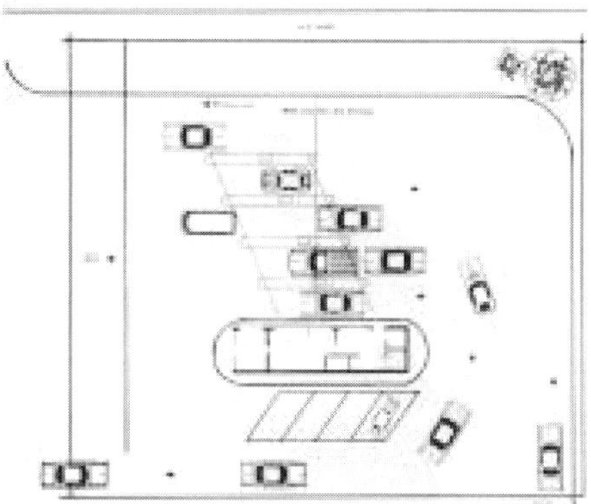

FREE STEEL TAPE MEASURE

With Deposit Transaction While Supply Lasts "Come . . . See How We Measure Up."

You save time with our new drive-up system

PLEASE NOTE: OUR DRIVE-UP WINDOWS AT THE MAIN OFFICE WILL NO LONGER BE IN OPERATION.

SOUTH OTTUMWA
SAVINGS BANK
OTTUMWA, IOWA 52501
FDIC
A FULL SERVICE BANK

The Motor Bank at 501 N. Weller opened in 1980 and operated until 2014.

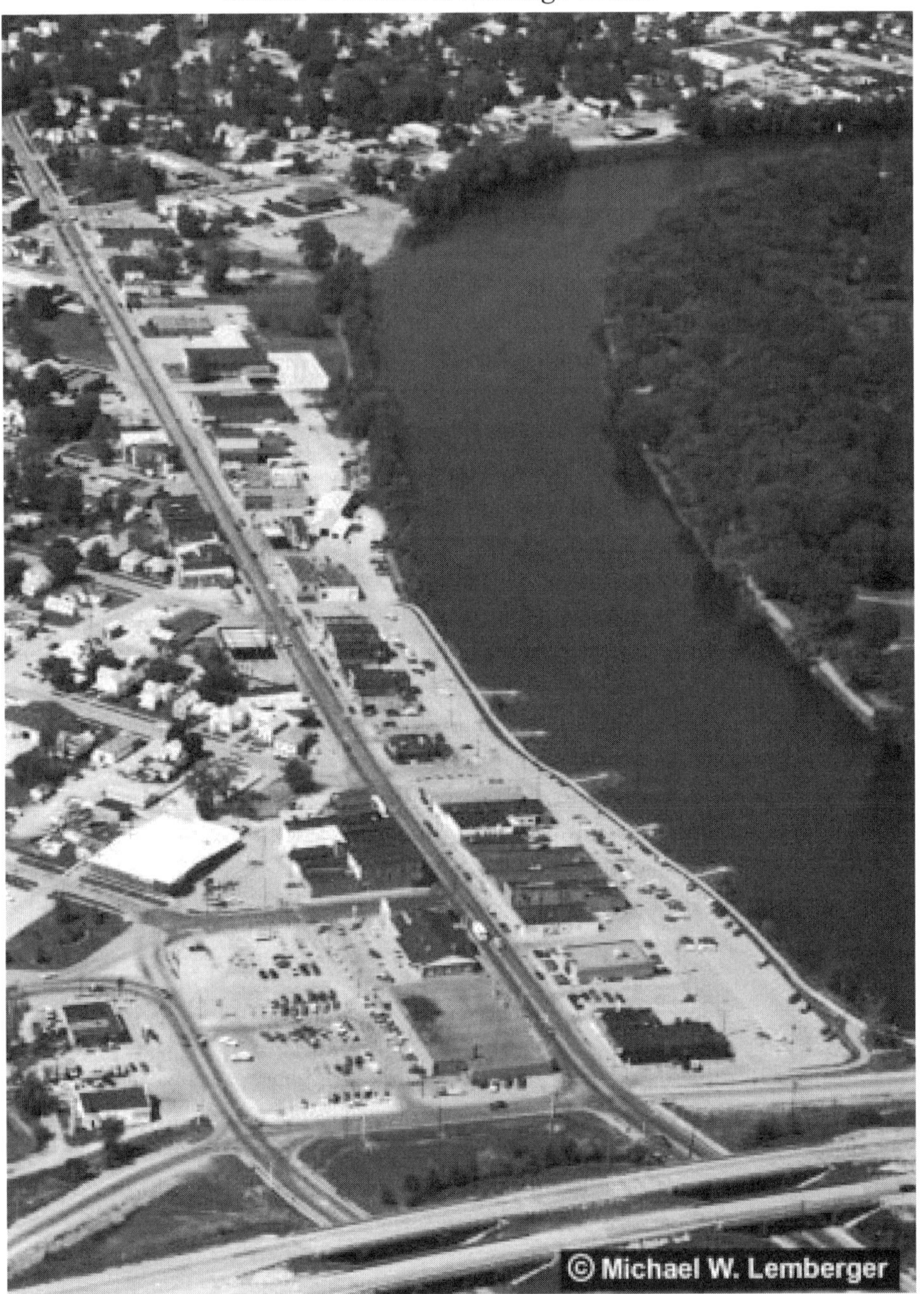

1988 aerial view of South Ottumwa. Highway 34 / 63 runs across the bottom of the photograph. Church Street runs diagonally from upper left to lower right. The Ottumwa Park lagoon is at right. South Ottumwa Savings Bank is near the bottom center, next to the Fareway grocery store.

Regular farm visits usually resulted in homemade desserts and iced tea. One resulted in an abundance of fleas, and we had to have the car fumigated.

-- Mike Miller

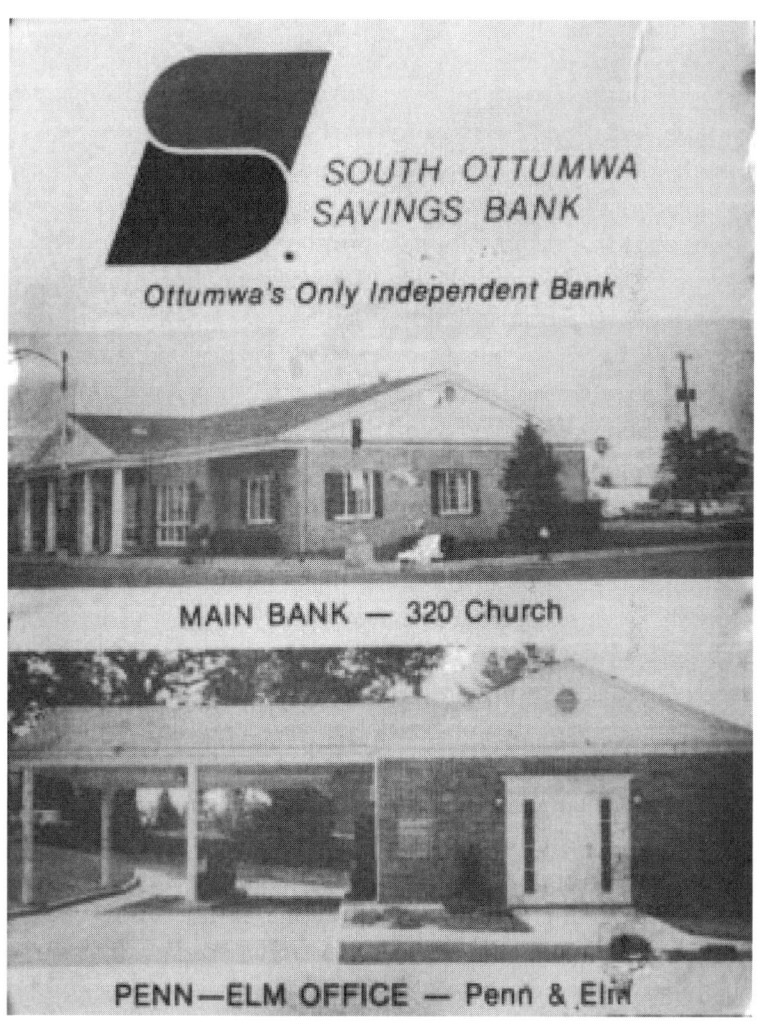

This color ad, showing the Main Bank and the northside office at the intersection of Pennsylvania Avenue and North Elm Street, formed the cover of an Ottumwa map given away about 1980.

South Ottumwa Savings Bank

South Ottumwa Savings Bank

Ottumwa's
Only
Home-Owned
Bank!

Same personal service and commitment to the community since the beginning in 1903... and on the same corner since the first building was erected in 1912! Depend on us to serve you for generations to come!

Member FDIC and an
Equal Opportunity Lender

Some of the many customer appreciation gifts the bank distributed.

Bank sale pends approval

South Ottumwa Savings priced at $7.8 million

In 1986, South Ottumwa Savings Bank was sold, with the majority of the stock purchased by a new corporation, South Ottumwa Bancshares Inc.

After the sale was finalized, Myron L. Ackley, president of the SOSB board of directors, retired from the Bank following a 30-year career. He joined South Ottumwa Savings Bank in 1955 as an executive vice president and member of the board of directors.

Robert (Bob) Ackley became president of the Bank in 1970 and chairman of the board in 1986. He retired in 1987 after 31 years with South Ottumwa Savings Bank.

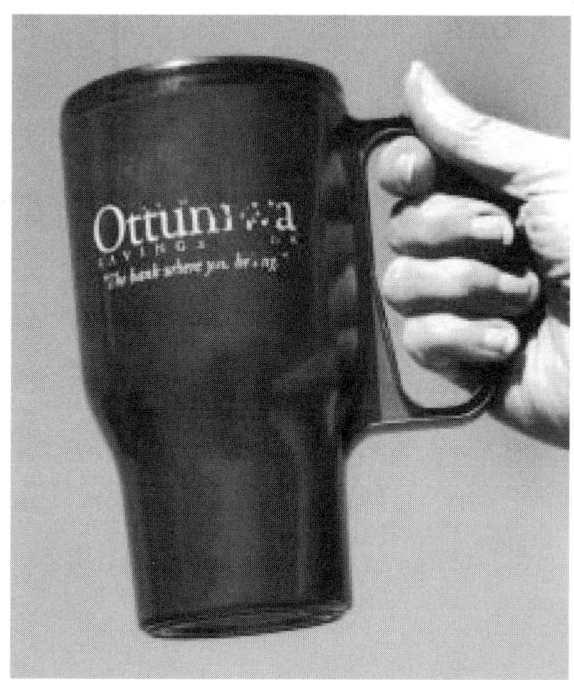

A travel mug was a favorite giveaway -- still used even when travel-worn.

South Ottumwa Savings Bank

Front row: Marcia Stam, Sue Shannon, Michele Bremer, Carole Black, Linda Reed. Back row: Tammy Kosman, Rae Albertson, Gary Johnson, Angie Rainbolt, Linda Bickford.

Bank bags through the years

The Sunshine Club

South Ottumwa Savings Bank's Sunshine Club was established in July 1990. Designed especially for customers 55 years of age or more, the Sunshine Club (originally the Sunshine Society) provides an unbeatable combination of banking services and opportunities for group travel and social events.

The Sunshine Club is not just a travel club – it's about fun and fellowship. Bank travel has focused on a variety of destinations, both domestic and international — from one day travels to overnights and extended stays.

The Sunshine Club is about the value of friendship and fun. It provides personal services with a financial and social

Early coin purse giveaway, when the club was the "Sunshine Society"

Being involved with the Sunshine Club since 1990 has taught me so much—the value of friendship and fun, humility, to appreciate the many blessings life has to offer, how to listen, the ability to be flexible...the list is endless.

-- Nancy McWilliams

Coin purse from the Sunshine Club

package – a great opportunity to have fun, make new friends, and renew acquaintances.

The Sunshine Club coordinates exceptional events with every detail arranged to include the fellowship, friends and fun that are the mission of the Club.

South Ottumwa Savings Bank is committed to supporting the community, plus we believe in always having a reason to celebrate. At South Ottumwa Savings Bank, seniority has its rewards, and the Sunshine Club offers something for everyone.

Our People Serving Southern Iowa
South Ottumwa Savings Bank

Bookkeeping Dept.: Left to right, Charlotte Brumbaugh; Melissa Replogle; Cheryl Schlotter; Jeanie Fredrickson, Head Bookkeeper; not pictured Cindy Walker.

Teller Dept.: Left to right, Beverly Miller; LaNelle Stamps; Barb Stevens; Kim Haines; Neena Lockett; Deb Robertson; Laura Goodvin; Lenora Gelse; Marcie Craver; not pictured, Marica Stam.

Branch Managers: Left to right, Sharon Shaw; Roberta Arnold.

AG Dept.: Left to right, Kathy Ebelsheiser; Lowell McCracken, Vice Pres.; not pictured Mary Ann Fisher.

Ottumwa's Only Home Owned Bank

Customer Service Dept.: Left to right, Imogene DeDecker; Connie Stufflebeam; Sue Shannon; Marilyn Watts, Asst. Vice Pres.; Gail Bainbridge, Asst. Cashier; Janet Ransom; Nancy McWilliams, Asst. Cashier/Sunshine Director; Rae Albertson.

Personal Loan Dept.: Left to right, Helen Walraven, Asst. Vice Pres.; Mike Miller, Vice Pres./Manager of PLD; Carol Bingaman; Joan West; Amanda Herlein; Virginia Steele.

Phil Drumm, President; Don Roemerman, Exec. Vice Pres.

320 Church St.

682-7541

MEMBER FDIC

Trust Dept.: Gary Johnson, Vice Pres/Trust Officer; Linda Reed; not pictured Linda Bickford.

Ottumwa *Courier* annual Progress Edition on March 21, 1992

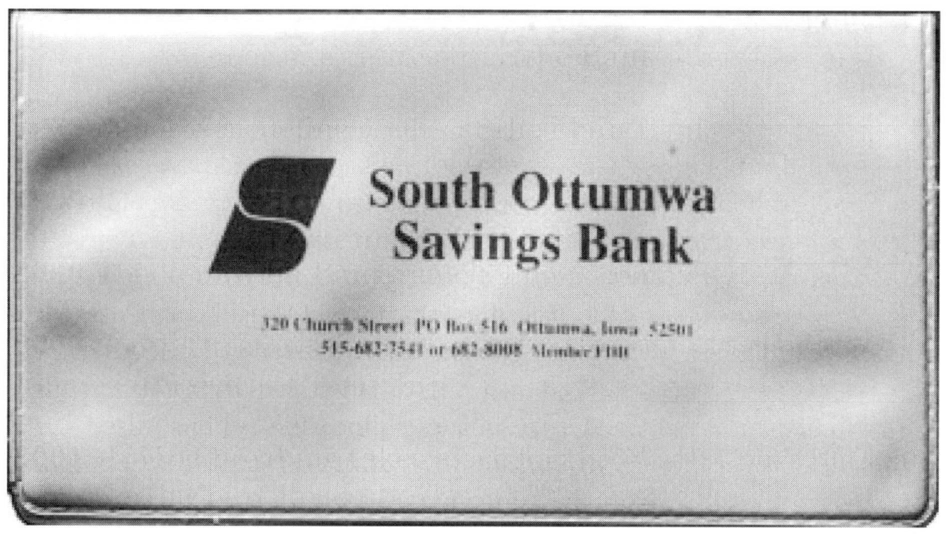

Checkbook cover from the 1990s

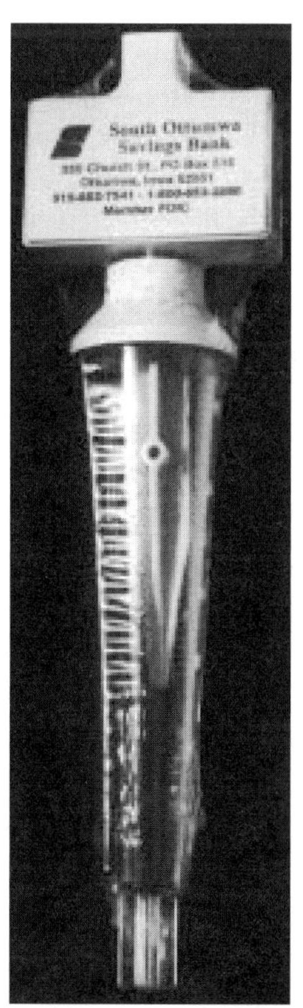

Computers in the bank were almost non-existent. We used microfiche (microfilm sheets) to look up customer balances in their accounts. We still used passbook savings account books that we manually kept up to date for our customers.

Our lobby closed at 2:00 p.m. each day, and we had a rope that we strung across the hall so customers had access only to our Personal Loan Department.

— Sue Shannon

Rain gauge given to customers in the 1990s

DECEMBER 31, 1993

ASSETS

Cash & Due From Banks		$ 4,283,500.50
U. S. Treasury Securities		6,373,124.73
Securities of Federal Agencies		30,411,731.42
Municipal Bonds		37,306,109.71
Other Securities		1,637,182.54
Fed Funds Sold		3,250,000.00
Loans	$45,602,725.91	
Allowance for Loan Losses	799,418.76	
Loans Net		44,803,307.15
Bank Premises & Furniture & Fixtures		298,384.52
Income Earned But Not Collected		1,308,628.48
Other Assets		47,233.07
TOTAL		$129,719,202.12

LIABILITIES

Deposits		$114,926,047.36
Capital	$ 669,600.00	
Surplus	1,830,400.00	
Undivided Profits	7,211,382.22	
Unrealized Appreciation Investment Securites	2,901,130.00	
Total Capital Accounts		12,612,512.22
Interest Earned But Not Paid		400,604.15
Other Liabilities		1,780,038.39
TOTAL		$129,719,202.12

EQUAL HOUSING LENDER

MEMBER

F.D.I.C.

Statement of the bank's financial condition as of December 31, 1993.

Once a good customer gave the bank a nice decorating tree for Christmas. Nancy McWilliams drove the truck to go pick it up, with Mike Miller and me riding in back trying to hold the tree upright. Nancy drove fast and it was difficult to stay in the truck, let alone trying to hold onto the tree.

--Lowell McCracken

During the 1970s, note payments were posted and logged manually, and the end of day balancing of the "work" was also done manually. With a pencil and an adding machine, the head teller logged the day's debits and credits to document the bank's position.

The banks in Ottumwa manually exchanged checks on a daily basis. A designated employee would board the bus with checks deposited or cashed at South Ottumwa Savings Bank from other financial institutions and deliver them to the proper place.

—Nancy McWilliams

Award presented to South Ottumwa Savings Bank in 1996 by Bauer Financial Reports Inc.

In 1992, South Ottumwa Savings Bank purchased Peoples Federal Savings and Loan, adding a large customer base to the bank. At that time Peoples was online (immediate transaction posting) but changed to batch processing. Everyone adjusted.

A computer was installed to run the Peoples system at South Ottumwa Savings Bank during conversion. When Lowell McCracken was looking for wiring to hook the computer up, he literally fell through the ceiling. We all had quite a scare, but he was fine. The computer did get set up, and memories of Lowell and the sky falling will last forever.

— Penny Reed

The Plainsman-Clarion--Thursday, March 27, 1997--Page 4

the fine medical care they make available to our area residents, Hospital is the [illegible] determined and dedicated staff, in Washington, phone 319- 653-5481, to our readers' attention.

South Ottumwa Savings Bank

No bank has done more to aid in the development of our area than the South Ottumwa Savings Bank. This is true not only because of the fact that they provide excellent banking services and employment opportunities for many of our local people, but also for the fact that they are a cornerstone in the financial community as well.

You would have to look very hard to find a more community minded bank. The prosperity and growth that our area enjoys is a direct result of their being a part of the financial strength of the many people who come in contact with South Ottumwa Savings Bank located at 320 Church in Ottumwa, phone (515)-682-7541 also on Pennsylvania and Elm through checking and savings accounts, loans, CD's, IRA's Safe Deposit boxes and more.

Due to the management's excellent capabilities, South Ottumwa Savings Bank continues to uphold their high standard of quality in their banking services, availability of jobs for local people and contribution toward the growth of our area.

Their position in the agricultural and industrial growth of our area is more than adequate reason to give them our unconditional gratitude. When you want more then "just a bank", just go to South Ottumwa Savings bank, that's "just" what you'll get.

A 1997 article from the Richland, Iowa *Plainsman-Clarion*

Contains $28 U.S. Currency

Above and left: This pencil is unique not only because of the dollar-sign shape but because it is actually made of $28 in retired U.S. currency.

Our Christmas parties were for employees only, no spouses.

I always enjoyed the South Ottumwa Boosters Open House, which was on the first Sunday after or before Thanksgiving. We participated by opening new Christmas club accounts and having Santa and Mrs. Santa here for the kids, along with cookies and punch for all. And we started handing out our calendars for the next year also.

-- Rae Albertson

Phil Drumm,
SOSB president
1987-1996

Phil Drumm was humble, with an incredible work ethic and a photographic memory. He always carried loan documents in his back pocket -- just in case -- and once was repossessing a car when the owner shot out the motor.

-- Lin Drumm

One of the saddest times at SOSB was in June of 1996 when the President of our bank Phil Drumm, member of the Board of Directors Dave Carpenter, and two other businessmen from Ottumwa were killed in a plane crash as they were coming home from a fishing trip. I will never forget the phone call I received around 2:00 a.m. Monday morning, telling me the news so we would all know before the morning news. I think we were all in a state of shock.

I really don't remember too much about the funeral, other than the church was full with standing room only, and we all wore our blue bank sweaters. Phil cared very much about the employees of the bank and his community. The huge turnout for his funeral was a great tribute to him. The history of our bank was totally changed with his death.

— Sue Shannon

June of 1996 was a tragic time for the Ottumwa community with the deaths of four prominent community leaders. One of those leaders was Phil Drumm, President of South Ottumwa Savings Bank.

In January 1997 I was proud and honored to become the next President and CEO of South Ottumwa Savings Bank. It was a transitional time for the community and the bank. It has always been my belief and also the bank's belief that community banks need to be positive forces within their communities.

The community of Ottumwa has seen many exciting improvements over the past few years and South Ottumwa Savings Bank has always been very proactive in leading the way.

South Ottumwa Savings Bank's success is the result of many dedicated professionals who are employed there. I want to congratulate the shareholders, directors, officers and staff of the bank for the vision to add the new addition and remodel the existing bank building. I wish South Ottumwa Savings Bank much success as it moves forward into the future.

— Thomas M. Awtry

Tom Awtry,
SOSB president
1997-2012

Vault money was supplied by Union Bank & Trust and transported in the back of a pickup truck. Money was delivered to other SOSB locations by different employees who were scheduled to work at the location. There was no armored car service.

The 1980s brought the age of technology, but only on an as-needed basis. The majority of the bank's transactions were still done manually, as were the management reports. Banking used to be less complicated and less competitive, and identity theft was a non-event.

— Nancy McWilliams

Jar opener -- a customer appreciation gift

Back in 1992, personal computers were pretty scarce in the bank. Phil Drumm purchased two computers, using one for his work and the other in the loan department. From that small beginning they became an item everyone got.

— Penny Reed

Then there was the time the crew thought the sky was falling in on them. The bank never threw anything away, even an old broken chair, and one member of the crew decided the attic was the place to put it. He climbed up to store the chair and stepped into open space in the ceiling, falling a good twenty feet to the main floor through electric wires, water pipes, and insulation. He landed standing up, still holding one leg of the broken chair.

--Lowell McCracken

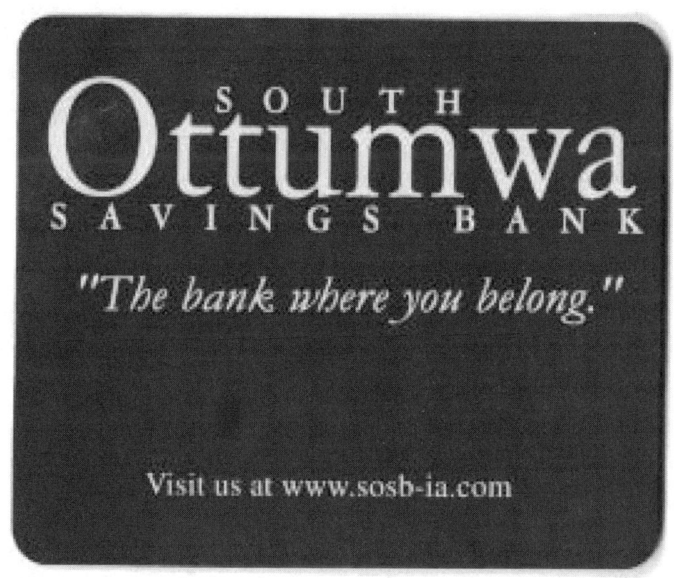

Mousepad -- a customer appreciation gift

Working at South Ottumwa Bank for 19 years has many memories for me, but remembering them after all this time may be a little difficult.

We were kind of like one big family – I started out as a teller and retired as head teller. It was mostly young tellers, so it was like being a mother to them, but they respected me and made it enjoyable for me.

—Margie Tennyson

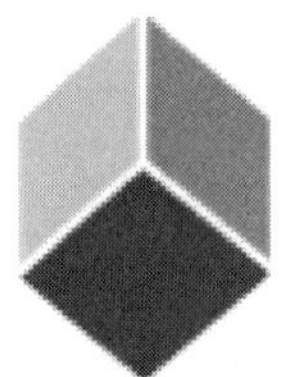

Building the North Court Bank

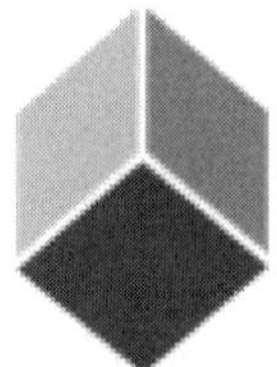

The vault is set in place before the building is constructed around it.

The North Court Bank was completed in 2002.

We manually posted to the general ledger, manually posted loan payments, and manually managed the loan portfolio. During my time at the bank I've survived the building of the two-story addition, building of the Motor Bank, remodeling of Penn-Elm Bank, building of the loan department, remodeling the Main Bank lobby, building the North Court Bank, and now the new addition and remodel of the Main Bank.

--Mike Miller

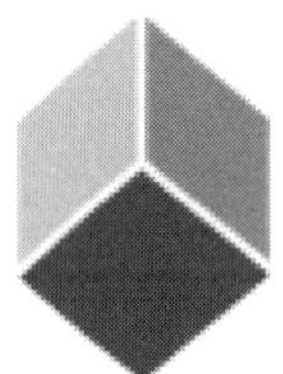

100 Years

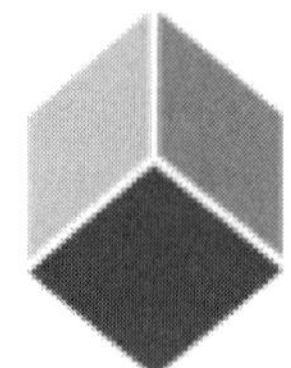

In 2003, South Ottumwa Savings Bank celebrated 100 years since its founding. Employees celebrated with several different promotions, including dressing up in old-style clothes and giving customers glass paperweights. Throughout the years, employees have always enjoyed getting into the spirit by dressing up for fun occasions.

Deposit Services Department in centennial garb. *Front row left to right:* Beth Van Engelenhoven, Marcia Stam, Don Agee. *Back row left to right:* Michele Bremer, Kathy Kearney.

Centennial logo, created to celebrate 100 years of service to the community

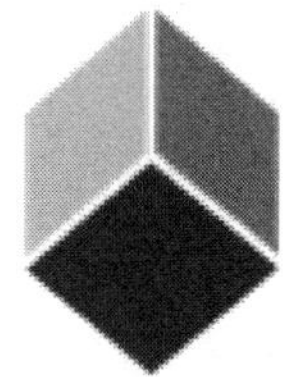

Fun, Games, and Community Service

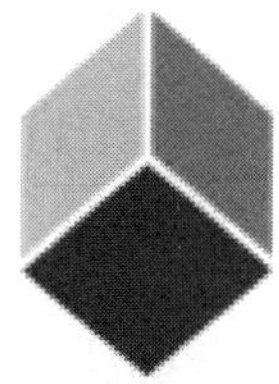

Tee shirt logo

The annual hog roast, with a hog donated by one of the crew, was held at the South Side Country Club or at Izaak Walton Club. All the spouses and board members were invited which made for a great evening in a casual way.

--Lowell McCracken

The Bank has hosted the annual Oktoberfest Kiddie Parade for more than 20 years, with several floats over the years. One of the employees' favorite events, it is always a great time.

We had hog roasts in the fall, and everyone was invited to them. Lowell McCracken would cook the hog and we would all bring a side dish.

— Rae Albertson

The bank has sent teams to the annual Junior Achievement SnoBowl fund raiser for many years. The team in 2005: *Front row:* Dawn Benedict, Tiffany Sloan. *Back row:* Susie Billings, Michele Bremer, Ginny Woodruff.

Mike Miller as Frank McIntire, president of the bank, and Pam Kaupins as Mrs. McIntire, in the Ottumwa Community Players annual Lantern Tour in Ottumwa Cemetery in 2003.

Back in the late 70s a crew of six to eight employees would seek out the best and the largest Christmas tree for the bank. That took us to a neat tree farm down in Davis County. Of course it would be very cold, windy, and sometimes snowy, but the crew was faithful and would always come back with the best find. One year it was extra cold with lots of snow on the ground, and the pickup we took to bring smaller trees for some of the employees died right at the farm and we had to get it towed back to town the next day.

It was always exciting to decorate the big tree and hear all the comments about how big it was!

--Lowell McCracken

South Ottumwa Savings Bank

From top:
Nancy McWilliams
Gary Johnson
Marilyn Watts
Rae Albertson
Sue Shannon
Linda Reed

The 2002 Celebration Ball, sponsored by the Sunshine Club at the Hotel Ottumwa. The club brought in a big band and even hired men from the Ottumwa Community Players to dance with the ladies.

In 2003, South Ottumwa Savings Bank sponsored a YMCA night in the winter. Employees could bring their families and enjoy the facilities plus enjoy pizza and pop. This is a family event that the bank enjoys providing occasionally for its employees.

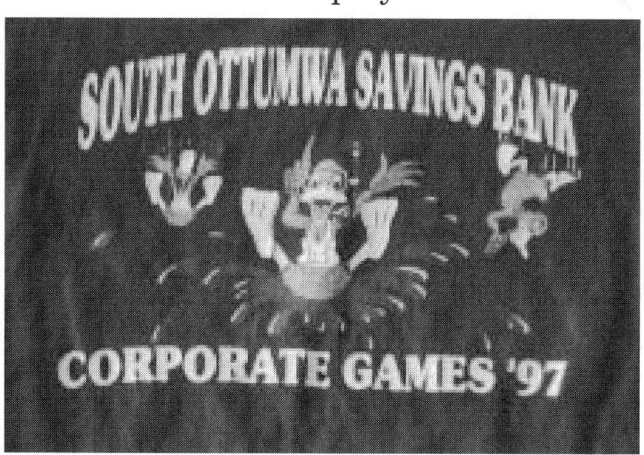

Bank president Phil Drumm organized the Youth Football League and created scholarships enabling everyone to participate. --Lin Drumm

A nice benefit of working at South Ottumwa Savings Bank is celebrating successes with parties, most held at Bridge View Center or the Hotel Ottumwa.

The Bank has always encouraged employee participation in community causes, including this team which raised money through the Alzheimer's Walk in 2011.

Race for the Cure team, one of many that Bank employees have formed through the years to support a cause they are passionate about -- breast cancer awareness and treatment.

Employees posing with their garbage bags at the start of an outing to help Make Ottumwa Shine.

The staff at Hedrick Bank in Hedrick, Iowa, celebrating Easter with an Easter Bonnet contest. Left to right: Susan Comstock, Kim Fears, Dianne Schuttlefield, Barb Echelberry.

Halloween is always fun, and who doesn't love to dress up? *Left to right:* Kamala Fisher, Earl Hanes, Janita Williams.

Employees dressed up for Cowboy Days, a celebration promoting a bull-riding event at Bridge View Center. *Left to right:* Melissa Rhoads, Barb Neill, Judy Black, Marcia Stam, Earl Hanes.

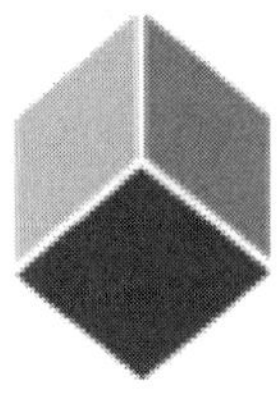

Duck Races

The Duck Races were an annual event to raise money for Ottumwa Regional Health Foundation, and every year South Ottumwa Savings Bank partnered to help sell duck adoptions and merchandise.

Bank president Phil Drumm was one of the organizers who brought the Duck Races to Ottumwa.

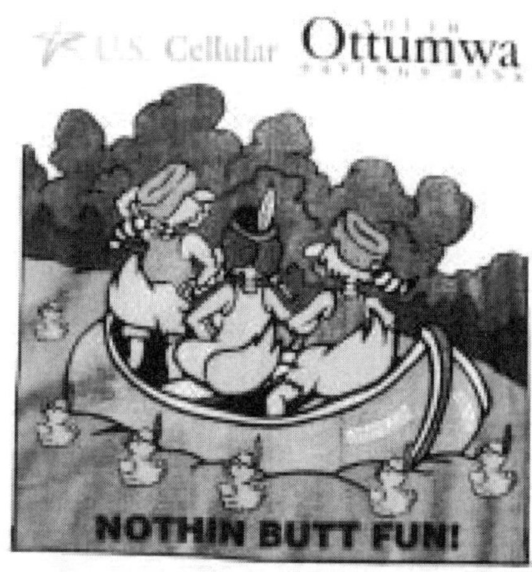

Graphic from the 1999 souvenir tee -- front and back

On a very warm Saturday, August 12, 2000, bank employees gathered and raised almost $300.00 for ORHC for a new ambulance. It was a beautiful day and as in past years, the water balloon slingshot was a huge success! There was a continual waiting line and all ages enjoyed trying to hit the target. We sold close to 1,300 duck adoptions and duck "stuff" in the bank prior to the duck race day.

—Pam Kaupins

Metal duck pins in various colors

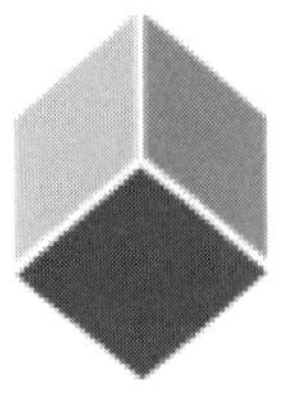

Sand in the City

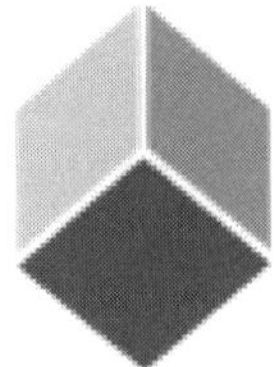

In 2006 the bank decided to sponsor a fun event called "Sand in the City". The event was held for three years.

A professional sand sculptor came to our small town to teach teams in creating and sculpting sand in a tournament setting.

Pam Kaupins asked if I would be co-captain alongside Scott Piper on the bank's team, made up of several people within our community. I thought it was a fun idea – I mean, how hard could building a sand castle be? WRONG! We went in for training. That sounds a little silly, training for building sand castles.

Bert (the professional sand sculptor) explained how we needed to build these large sculptures. We had to figure out how big our base formation needed to be compared to the amount of sand we were allotted. Then he showed us how to wet the sand and pound it within the base formation to create a solid block of sand. Then you removed the base formation and it was time to start sculpting. This was really a lot more than putting sand in a bucket and flipping the bucket over to create the beginning of a castle! Everything had to be just right!

We practiced several times before the big tournament. Sculpting sand is very different than sculpting clay. With clay if you accidently cut a little too much off, all you had to do is attach more clay and continue. With sand, if you make a mistake, you have to rethink your sculpture.

It was a great experience and a lot of fun. The year we participated in the event we won first place – it was so exciting! I am glad I was chosen to participate in this fun event. It is definitely an experience I will cherish.

—Kista Applegate

The bank's winning sculpture

Fan given out to promote the 2006 Sand in the City competition

These miniature clay models were used to plan the full-scale sculpture. The models are on display at the Main Bank.

South Ottumwa Savings Bank

Our bank team worked hard, acquired teambuilding skills, camaraderie, and declared it was a great experience. This event was created to raise corporate dollars for Bridge View Center Arts and Entertainment. The first year, 11 teams competed to build a sand sculpture to be judged -- and Kista led the way to the bank winning the grand prize. The event drew many people from other parts of Iowa (and other states). Iowa Lieutenant Governor Sally Pederson presented us with a certificate of recognition.

It was Sandsational!

--Pam Kaupins

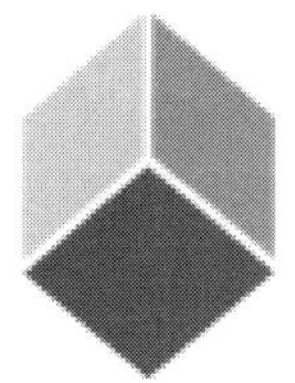

Live After Five

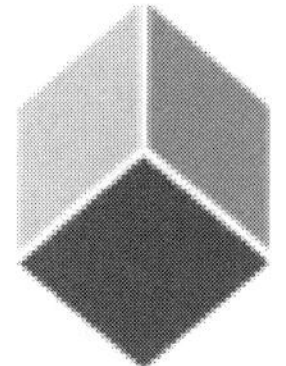

South Ottumwa Savings Bank started this community event in 2001 at the beautiful Central Park in downtown Ottumwa. Designed for the entire family, throughout the seasons it has brought wonderful free entertainment to the families who gather in Central Park.

Each Friday for four weeks in July, we present a band on the stage and the Hotel Ottumwa provides an opportunity for beverages and food.

A medley of Live After Five tee shirts through the years.

We give away prizes during the band's break time and recently have had Heartland Humane Society dogs parade across the stage, enabling the organization to increase its adoptions.

Many groups have participated in fund raisers throughout the years. We welcome the partnerships, whether non-profit groups or business sponsors.

Live After Five is one of the highlights of summertime in Ottumwa and many people look forward to it including class reunions who like to start their "kick off" weekend in the park.

A panoramic view of the Live After Five crowd, July 18, 2014

The Christmas parties were always a good time. President Bob Ackley was a big fan of the California Raisin commercial. So we decided to surprise him one year and four of us dressed up in black garbage bags, dark sunglasses, white gloves, and black tights and did a commercial that involved a dance. It was the first time we wore garbage bags to the Christmas party.

—Gail Bainbridge

South Ottumwa Savings Bank had one of the largest student loan programs in the area back in the 1990s. The bank was deeply involved in the community by providing student loans. The government took over the program and South Ottumwa Savings Bank had to sell the loans, so student loans were history.

— Penny Reed

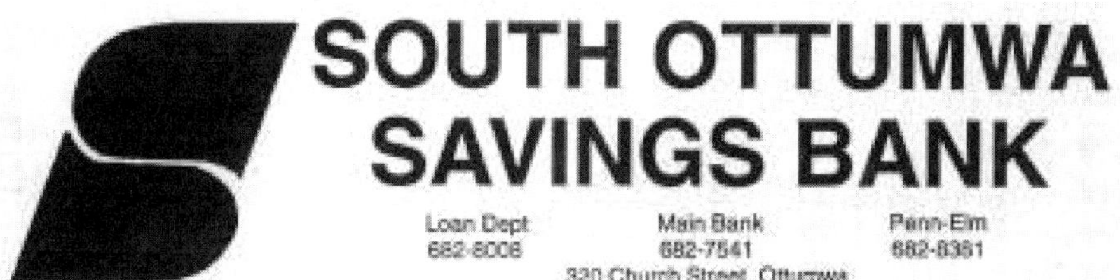

SOUTH OTTUMWA
SAVINGS BANK
Loan Dept
682-8006
Main Bank
682-7541
Penn-Elm
682-8361
320 Church Street Ottumwa

The "big S" logo which South Ottumwa Savings Bank used for a number of years was designed by bank president Phil Drumm's mother, Virginia (Jinny) Drumm.

Meet 1/2 of the Best Financial Team in SE Iowa

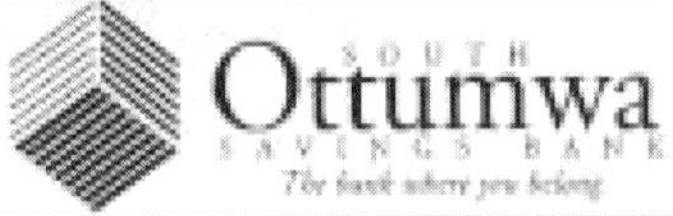

Member FDIC

South Ottumwa Savings Bank ad in the annual Ottumwa *Courier* Progress edition in 2012, just after the Bank purchased Hedrick Savings Bank and added HSB employees to the South Ottumwa Savings Bank family.

I remember Tammy our ATM machine — though I don't remember the whole jingle, I do recall the part about "She's easy."

— Rae Albertson

Meet the other 1/2 of the Best Financial Team in SE Iowa

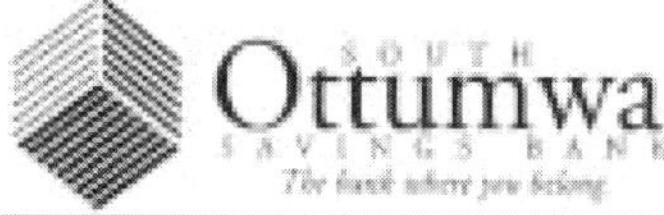

Member FDIC

During the farm crisis the farm department got a great surprise when Iowa State University gave them an award for being outstanding listeners and caring for the farmers in the area.

-- Lowell McCracken

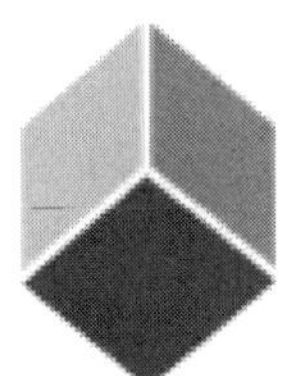

Adding to the Main Bank 2014

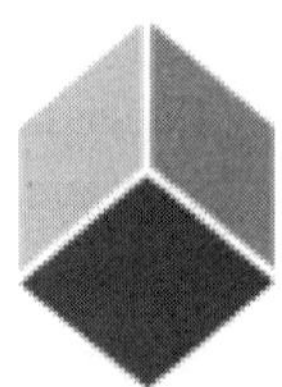

Above and right: The older section of the bank remained

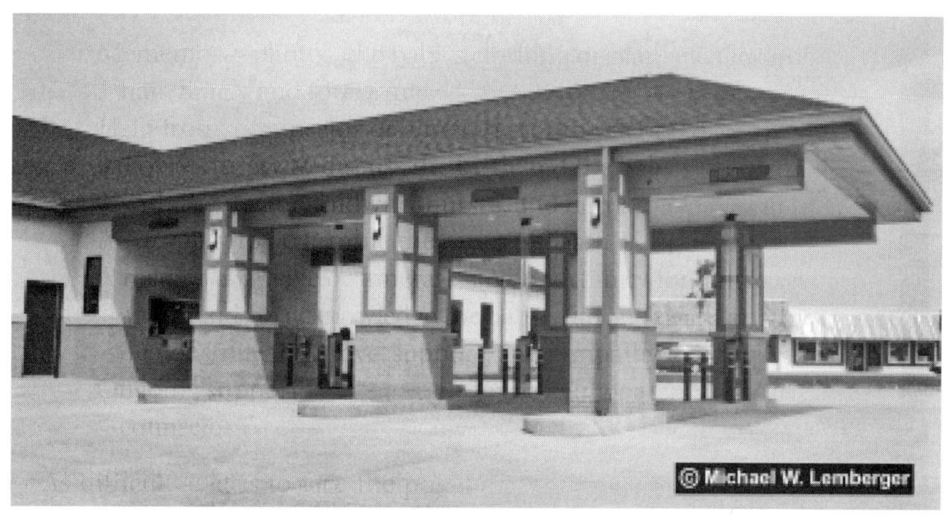

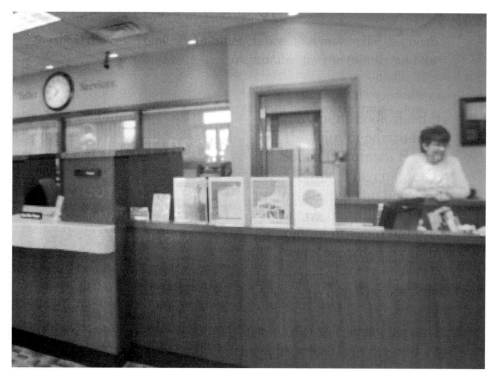

in operation as the new section was constructed.

New construction -- April 9, 2014

Construction progresses -- June 16, 2014

I imagine it was an inconvenience and maybe a challenge for the workers as well as the employees, who needed to walk through the maze of hanging wires, dangling lights and cords and equipment strewn on the floor. We have endured dust and more dust, odd construction odors from soldering fumes to carpet glue, loud music and even singing.

After our "isolation" plastic wall came down we felt like we were part of civilization again.

--Linda Reed

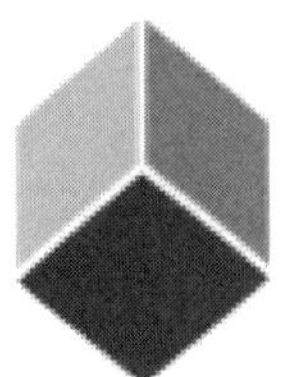

Remodeling the Old Bank

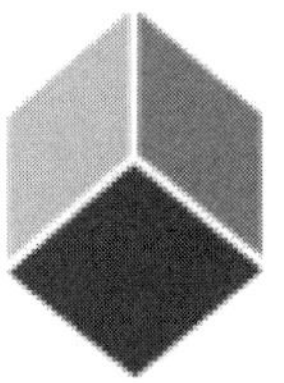

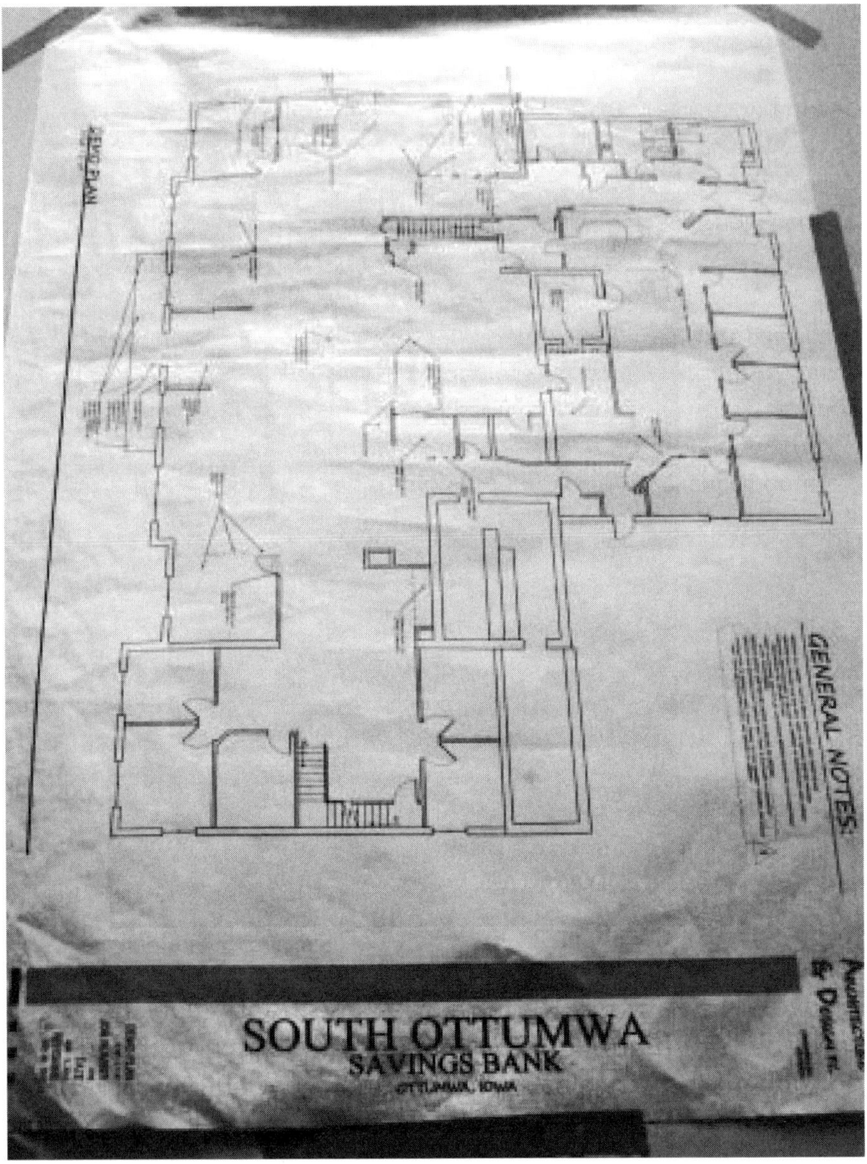

Floor plans detailing the renovation to be done in the 1964 section of the bank.

Light fixtures in the older section of the bank still provide illumination though the ceiling has been removed.

Workers tear up carpeting in the older section of the South Ottumwa Savings Bank.

Above: Richard Dye, project manager for the South Ottumwa Savings Bank expansion and remodeling. The contractor was Christner Construction of Ottumwa.

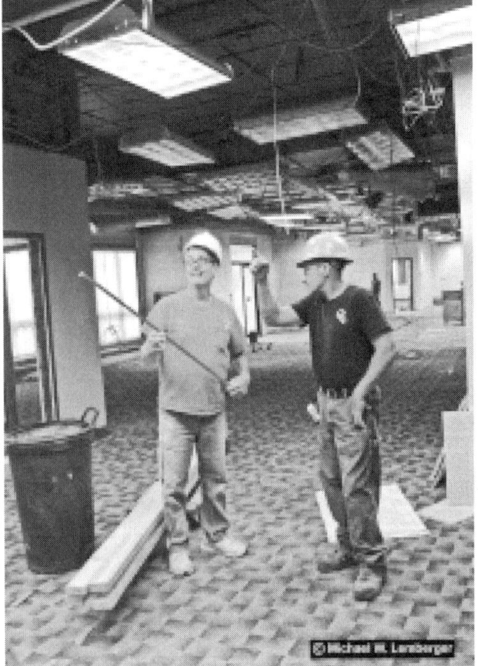

Left: Project manager Richard Dye instructs a worker regarding the remodeling of the older section of the bank building.

In the 1990s there was a fireplace in the lobby. Somehow a bird got caught in the chimney. Carol Bingman (the animal lover she was) would not let a bird suffer from being trapped in the chimney. She worked so hard, saved the bird, and let him fly out the front door.

— Penny Reed

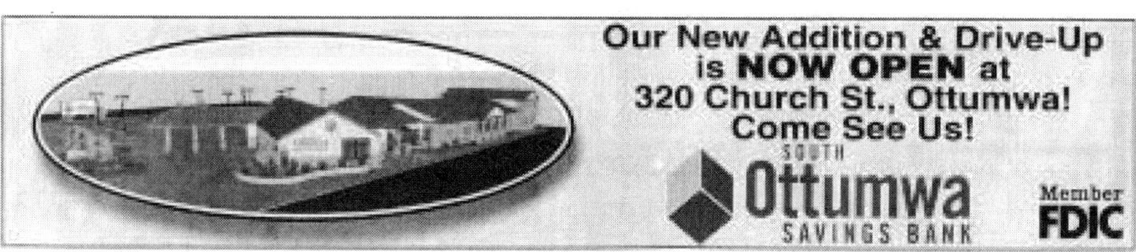

Advertisement in the Ottumwa *Courier* announcing the opening of the new addition and drive-up facility.

South Ottumwa Savings Bank

Tee-shirt logo

The lines between branches [connecting the computer terminals] were slow, so at least twice a week someone would call the main bank and we would have to go upstairs where the server was to unplug it to clear the lines, then count to 20 and plug it back in.

—Gail Bainbridge

© Michael W. Lemberger

Safe deposit boxes at the Main Bank.

Teri Messerschmitt
SOSB president, 2013-present

It is unbelievable how much banking has changed over the past 100 years! South Ottumwa Savings Bank has been a strong bank and a strong leader in the community and has stepped up and embraced the changes that have taken place throughout the years. This philosophy has resulted in tremendous growth during the bank's first 100 years.

South Ottumwa Savings Bank is very proud to be the only locally-owned bank in our community. We care about our customers, and we listen to our customers' feedback regarding their banking. South Ottumwa Savings Bank is very excited about continuing to grow with our customers by offering banking products that fit our customers' needs.

As technology changes, obviously we need to keep pace to be competitive. But we will never compromise our values, values established in the past that will continue to drive us forward into the future. We respect our past, we respect today and we will continue to respect our community as we work towards our next 100 years.

It is hard to imagine what changes we will see over the next 100 years of banking, but South Ottumwa Savings Bank is looking forward to continuing to be a strong leader in our community for many years to come!

—Teri Messerschmitt

For more information about these and other books, calendars and products, visit

www.pbllimited.com

PBL Limited
P.O. Box 935
Ottumwa Iowa 52501

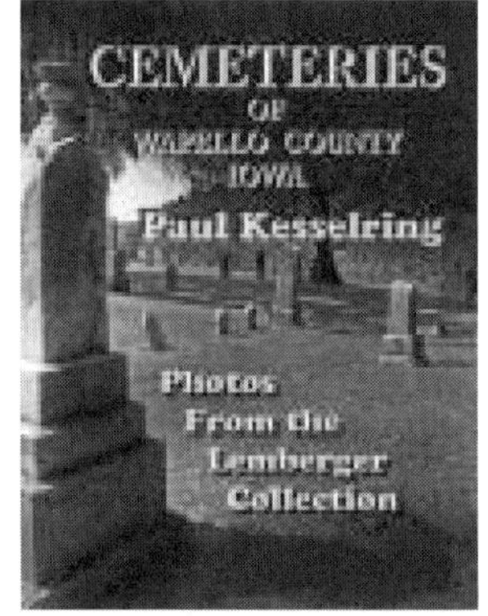